IMA
of America

SAN FRANCISCO
POLICE DEPARTMENT

MW00809778

This 1970s image shows SFPD officers on Powell Street with a cable car in the background. Years later, MUNI Cable Car operator Carl Payne, a 10-time cable car bell ringer winner, left his job at age 47 to become a SFPD officer. (Courtesy of San Francisco History Center, San Francisco Public Library.)

This solo officer poses on a Harley Davidson near the Golden Gate Bridge, c. 1970. (Courtesy of SFPD.)

MISSION STATEMENT

We, the members of the San Francisco Police Department, are committed to excellence in law enforcement and are dedicated to the people, traditions, and diversity of our City. In order to protect life and property, prevent crime, and reduce the fear of crime, we will provide service with understanding, response with compassion, performance with integrity, and law enforcement with vision.

IMAGES
of America

SAN FRANCISCO
POLICE DEPARTMENT

John Garvey

ARCADIA

DEDICATION

This book is dedicated to the memory of the officers of the SFPD who have died in the line of duty, as well as to those who have died as a result of their injuries off duty or were murdered off duty (these are not considered line-of-duty deaths). Also to SFPD officers injured and disabled in the line of duty.

I especially dedicate this to my great-great uncle SFPD Policeman Edward Maloney, star # 146, who was shot in the line of duty and died the late evening of April 19, 1915 at the corner of Sacramento and Davis Streets. His grave at Mission Santa Clara Cemetery has a tombstone engraved with 24 shamrocks. His killer Charles Felker (Anton Staninakis), alias Carl Fisher #24847, was sentenced to life in prison in San Quentin and his companion Otto Walker #24848 was sentenced to 10 years at San Quentin.

An old red scrapbook sat in the hallway closet of my parents home during my youth. It showed that Edward was one of 10 children, 7 boys and 3 girls, and 5 of the boys became policemen, 4 in San Francisco and 1 in Denver. The yellowish press clipping stated his last words to his partner Special Policeman Samuel McCain were "My God Sam, he got me." Officer Maloney never returned home to his wife, Anna, and six-month-old son Thomas Edward on Clement Street. His last watch ended that night at age 32 and he is memorialized like other fallen officers, on the City of San Francisco Memorial Wall (Hall of Justice) and State of California Memorial (Sacramento); and the National Law Enforcement Memorial, Panel 20, E3 in Washington, D.C.

To my grandmother, Mary Maloney, whom I called Nana. When I was eight years old she gave me a police alabaster whistle that belonged to her father, Joseph P. Maloney. I blew it a few times in front of Nana, and treasured it, and promised not to lose it. My grandmother died shortly thereafter and the old scrapbook and the whistle, led to my curiosity and to this book. I also dedicate this book to the memory of my cousin former SFPD Police Chief Michael Mitchell.

Last, I dedicate this book to Jeffery Fontana my former co-worker at the San Francisco 49ers Headquarters in Santa Clara. In October of 2001, Officer Jeffery Fontana of the San Jose Police Department (SJPD) was gunned down during a routine traffic stop. Today people can remember his service and honor him, as they enjoy Jeffery Fontana Park in San Jose, California.

CONTENTS

COVER IMAGE. SFPD officers are in formation for the funeral of their brother, bluecoat Edward Maloney, star 146, in this somber April 1915 San Francisco street scene.

ACKNOWLEDGMENTS

The author would like to thank members of the SFPD, current and retired, along with their families and survivors, who assisted with this project.

Thank you to retired SFPD Chief Tony Ribera for his willingness to help preserve history and for his outstanding idea to start the SFPD Citizens Police Academy. To Lt. Ken Cottura and the other members of the SFPD who educated me at the SFPD Citizens Police Academy #4 and to the members of Northern Station, who made my ride-along a most memorable event in 1996. To retired Deputy Chief Kevin Mullen, police historian, for taking personal time back in the early 1990s and speaking voluntarily to the City Guides training classes to educate us about the city's tremendous police history. And to Sgt. Robert Fitzer, director of the SFPD Museum and Archives, for helping me locate a group family photo of the Maloney police brothers. To my sister Judith Garvey, an assistant district attorney with the City of San Francisco, who was an inspiration.

In addition, I thank Jo-Ellen Radetich, who shared many items belonging to her beloved brother Richard, who was assassinated in the line of duty in 1970 in the Haight-Ashbury district. Jo-Ellen has spent her life keeping his memory alive in the form of memorials, committee work with other survivors of law enforcement deaths, and as a member of Bay Area Law Enforcement Families (BALEF).

Thanks goes to Patricia Akre, photographic curator, John Eby, and the rest of Susan Goldstein's staff at the San Francisco Public Library History Room. Thanks also goes to Erica Nordmeier, photographic duplication coordinator at the Bancroft Library at the University of California at Berkeley. I also thank the helpful archivists at the Gerald R. Ford Library in Ann Arbor, Michigan, Kenneth G. Hafeli and Helmi Raaska, who located U.S. Secret Service assassination attempt photographs for me as well as presidential correspondence.

In addition, I am grateful to Peter Fairfield and his staff at Gamma Photo Lab in San Francisco, who did an outstanding job with their professional black-and-white reproductions, as well as to the staffs at Kinko's and Wolf-Ritz Cameras.

To the staff at Arcadia Publishing in San Francisco, Chicago, and Charleston, I am thankful, especially to editor John Poultney and publisher Christine Talbot.

INTRODUCTION

If one does an Internet search on the San Francisco Police Department, or its acronym "SFPD," one may form a false opinion that the SFPD is spiraling out of control. For example, in 2004 the *San Francisco Chronicle* on its front page presents the department as being on a "roller coaster" ride over the last decade, saying it is in "crisis" mode. In 1993, critics pointed out what was wrong with the department by making in-house training videos such as "Lifestyles of the Poor and Lazy." In 1994, the *San Francisco Examiner* in a bold header wrote, "SFPD Hiring Too Many Bad Apples." The attacks on the SFPD are relentless, and the media has been the first to find fault with the SFPD. Compliments in recent years have been rare, and emphasis has been on the negative. Because of this, one SFPD officer lamented that the only thing the local newspapers were good for was toilet tissue.

Internet stories are rampant with several high-profile cases over the last decade concerning the top brass in several alleged actions: cover-up, sexual harassment, writing a questionable résumé of qualifications, public intoxication, and driving a motor vehicle under the influence. One can learn about a 2004 lawsuit filed by a former chief of police for $33 million against the City of San Francisco for his medical situation. Another chief, in 1992, was fired by the police commission after just 42 days on the job for allegedly having a few of his cops pull issues of the *Bay Times* from the street racks. The newspaper had written an unfavorable article about him and published an image of this particular chief holding a nightstick between his legs in a suggestive manner. The *Bay Guardian* published a Dolezal cartoon in 2004 showing a former police chief fighting with his son, a former officer—the latter with his right hand on the father's throat and a gun pointed at the father's head and the father with a knife in his right hand pointed at his son's head and a broken bottle in his left hand. This violent incident never happened. The press distorted reality and did a great disservice to the SFPD. The latter paper also referred to the force as having "cowboy cops."

A miniscule few rank-and-file officers have been accused of several alleged actions including shoplifting, suspect abuse, improper use of a nightstick and pepper spray, cheating at the academy (instructors providing students with answers), wrongful deaths, and sexual activity while on duty. The media has enthusiastically reported these incidents, going back to April 1984 and the infamous Rathskeller case, in which a young recruit who was partying was handcuffed and provided with sexual attention by a prostitute allegedly paid for by some officers. A female officer stepped forward to report the incident and later filed a $2 million harassment suit.

Then there was "Fajitagate," the off-duty November 2002 street brawl incident when then San Francisco District Attorney Terence Hallinan, who later sent the case to a grand jury, stated on a television news program that the police department's investigation of the fight "hadn't been handled as an ordinary case" and had "almost Watergate aspects to it." Peter Keane, dean of the Golden Gate University School of Law, said "this was the first time since the Boss Tweed era in the 1870s in New York City that the entire top commanders of a big city police department had faced criminal charges." Later, when the facts were fully known, the mug shots taken of these high-ranking SFPD officials were destroyed by court order.

Back in 1864, the SFPD was fortunate to have journalists such as Mark Twain (Samuel Clemens) reporting in the San Francisco papers accurate accounts of police activity. However, things changed in the late 20th and early 21st centuries. I have learned again and again as a historian to be suspicious of things in the newspaper or on the internet and to never judge a person's character and career on one incident—or alleged incident. In the majority of these incidents, if one follows them through to the end, one will discover the officers were unfairly accused and exonerated on all charges.

Given this, my purpose is not to write another piece that plays the blame game and drags the department through the mud. My purpose is to bring to light the fine traditions and the outstanding women and men of the SFPD. I hope you will enjoy this book about the brave people we call San Francisco Police Officers. Only a few are chosen to wear the famed seven-point star or the patrol special six-point Star of David which, by the way, are never called badges.

When my San Francisco home was burglarized in 1985, the responding officer quipped, "Crime never takes a holiday in San Francisco." He was absolutely correct, as you will discover. The SFPD have a bumper sticker and a poster that reads, "Thank God for the TAC squad." As a native San Franciscan who has seen the SFPD in action my entire life, I say "Thank God for the SFPD."

Let us now honor their service and be thankful for their commitment and willingness to sacrifice their lives for us in the line of duty. During the course of my research on the San Francisco Police Department, I found thousands of examples of heroism and am proud to present some of those to you now.

One

1849–1900

Malachi Fallon was one of six early San Francisco police chiefs known as marshals. Fallon was born in County Athlone, Ireland, in 1814 and emigrated to America with his family as a young boy. He grew up in New York City and ran a saloon as well as served as a jailer at the Tombs Prison. Fallon came to San Francisco during the Gold Rush in 1849 and was appointed city marshal, receiving a $6,000 salary. Initially, the SFPD had no training, equipment, or uniforms. Their first office was a pre–Gold Rush schoolhouse in Portsmouth Square. The city's marshals were Malachi Fallon (1850–1851, 1852–1853), R.G. Crozier (1851–1852), W.C. Thompson (part of 1852), Brandt Sequine (1853), John W. McKenzie (1854), and Ham North (1855). (Courtesy of San Francisco History Center, San Francisco Public Library.)

J. McElroy served as police chief for part of 1856 and was followed by James F. Curtis from 1856 to 1857. Police Chief Martin J. Burke, shown here, served from 1858 to 1866. During his stint as police chief, the SFPD became the first police department in the nation to use photography in police work. (Courtesy of San Francisco History Center, San Francisco Public Library.)

These two pistols were believed to have been used in the historic duel between U.S. Senator David C. Broderick and California State Supreme Court Justice David S. Terry on September 12, 1895. The duel, considered the last one fought in the State of California, almost did not happen. As preparations were being made for the duel Chief of Police Martin Burke and a couple of officers arrested the principals and brought them before Justice of the Peace Henry Coon, who discharged them on the ground that no actual misdemeanor had been committed. Despite fruitless efforts made by friends on both sides, the men squared off again the next day at the same location, a little over the line in San Mateo County, and Terry won. Although he was indicted and tried in San Rafael, he was ultimately acquitted. In December 1963, these famous pistols, set in a wood case with 19 pieces of loading and cleaning equipment, were reported missing from the Wells Fargo Bank History Room. They were recovered and were most recently sold by Butterfield and Butterfield at auction. (Courtesy of San Francisco History Center, San Francisco Public Library.)

Patrick Crowley was one of the city's early pioneers. In his youth he pulled boats on the waterfront for the ship captains. Later he was elected constable and then served as San Francisco police chief from 1866 to 1873 and from 1879 to 1897. Crowley initially had a force of less than 100 men to deal with riots and gangs such as the Sons of Freedom, the Revolutionary Committee, the Potrero Toughs, and the Sandlotters. The Sons of Freedom were broken up after several members of Crowley's force infiltrated the secretive group that met around a skull at midnight at Market and Ninth Streets to plan their ghoulish crimes. The Revolutionary Committee operated out of a den at Lombard and Montgomery Streets producing bombs, but Crowley stopped them as well. The Potrero Toughs hung out in the sand dunes and creek and were anti-Chinese. When the Sandlotters were making inroads in the city government Crowley threaten to arrest the mayor himself. Crowley died on May 10, 1929. (Courtesy of San Francisco History Center, San Francisco Public Library.)

George Washington Hogue joined the SFPD in 1876. Born in Summit County, Ohio, in 1832, he joined the Sacramento Rangers in August 1861 as part of Company F, 2nd Volunteer Calvary and spent most of the Civil War at the Benicia Arsenal. Before he joined the SFPD he was a longshoreman. In 1880, after only four years on the force, he resigned due to heart problems and died in 1890. (Courtesy of San Francisco History Center, San Francisco Public Library.)

The famous Chinatown squad, posing in front of 25 Taylor Street in 1895, included, from left to right, officers J.M. Gee, Coleman, police clerk August Pistolesi, Sergeant Price, Moriarity, and J.M. Murry. (Courtesy of San Francisco History Center, San Francisco Public Library.)

In 1886 C.W. Armanger went to Irvin Jachen to request a seven-pointed star, which represents the seven seals in the Book of Revelation in the New Testament and include virtue, divinity, prudence, fortitude, honor, glory, and praising God. The star was adopted by the police force to remind everyone of the precepts by which the police are guided. The first SFPD policeman to wear a star was Isaiah W. Lees, who wore the six-pointed Star of David in 1853, which evolved into a five-pointed star, then into the seven-pointed star. The star is always worn on the left breast, traditionally the vulnerable part of the body. This image shows the various stars of SFPD regulars. Numbers continue to be important for some officers today. Many Asian officers prefer to have an eight on their star, which is considered lucky. They do not want a four because in Japanese, the number four is shi, which also means "death." (Courtesy of San Francisco History Center, San Francisco Public Library.)

Two
1901–1950

Police Chief William Sullivan Jr. (1900–1901) had a force that was on duty for 6 hours, then off for 6 hours, worked another 6 hours, and then had 12 hours off. This schedule was in use as early as 1895 and possibly even earlier under previous chiefs Theodore G. Cockrill (1874–1876), Henry H. Ellis (1876–1877), John Kirpatrick (1878–1879), and Isaiah W. Lees (1898–1900). (Courtesy San Francisco History Center, San Francisco Public Library.)

George Wittman served as police chief from 1901 to 1905. Notice the seven-pointed star floral arrangement above his head. Wittman was a tinsmith and joined the SFPD in 1884. While chief he personally led raids on gambling and opium dens in Chinatown, but the city administration opposed him for such vigorous law enforcement. He is buried in Alameda. (Courtesy of San Francisco History Center, San Francisco Public Library.)

This photograph shows the Hall of Justice prior to its destruction in the great earthquake and fire of 1906. (Courtesy of San Francisco History Center, San Francisco Public Library.)

In this image a San Francisco police officer directs a clean-up crew after the 1906 earthquake and fire. Following the quake, Mayor Eugene E. Schmitz issued the following proclamation: "The Federal Troops, the members of the Regular Police Force and all Special Police Officers have been authorized by me to KILL any and all persons engaged in Looting or the Commission of Any Other Crime . . . " A 2003 fictional book on this natural disaster has done a disservice to the SFPD by asserting that a large number of citizens were shot by police as looters. The reality was that only a few were shot, not the unsubstantiated 500 claimed on promotional tours by the book's author. (Courtesy of San Francisco History Center, San Francisco Public Library.)

James Thomas Graham, star 237, was born in 1874 and was a member of the SFPD from 1900 until his death in 1935. Both his brothers, George and Robert Graham, were also San Francisco cops. James's beat was in the South of Market Area along Second Street, an area hit hard by the 1906 earthquake and where much of the looting occurred. (Courtesy of Tom Graham.)

Park Station officers, pictured here *c.* 1906, included John "Jack" Lynch (front row, second from right). Lynch was shot in the neck during the robbery of the Haight Street Theatre and survived. (Courtesy of Tom Rey, SFFD Truck No. 1.)

COPYRIGHT 1907
By A. L. Murat

Police Chief Jeremiah F. Dinan (1905–1907) is shown in the first police car in the history of the SFPD. Notice the steering wheel on the right. In 1907 the SFPD was one of the first in the nation to use fingerprinting as a means of identification. Policemen hired at this time had to know their reading, writing, and arithmetic. The four math problems in Part 3 of the June 1907 exam were as follows: (1) add 94,592 + 76,259 + 68,542 + 3,007 + 87; (2) subtract 79,907 from 961,406; (3) divide 476,672 by 107; and (4) multiply 59,764 by 447. (Courtesy of San Francisco History Center, San Francisco Public Library.)

On the night of November 30, 1908, Police Chief William Biggy (1907–1908) took the police launch across the bay to Belvedere to confer with Police Commissioner Hugo Kiel. Biggy and engineer Murphy were the only people aboard the launch. They started back from Belvedere about 11:20 p.m., but when the launch reached the dock in San Francisco, Biggy was not on board. On December 14 his body was found floating near Goat Island. There was speculation, but never any verification, as to whether Biggy committed suicide or whether he was accidentally washed overboard. (Courtesy of San Francisco History Center, San Francisco Public Library.)

Jesse Brown Cook (1860–1938) was a member of the San Francisco Police Department from the 1890s to the 1930s and chief of police from 1908 to 1910. He began as a beat cop, then rose through the ranks to become sergeant of the Chinatown Squad. After retiring as chief of police he later returned to the force as police commissioner. Before joining the police force he studied taxidermy; worked as a sailor, drayman, and butcher; and toured Europe as a contortionist. His police career began in San Antonio and San Diego before he relocated to San Francisco. Cook compiled thousands of photographs and clippings into a unique portrayal of early 20th-century San Francisco; the collection is housed at the Bancroft Library, UC Berkeley. (Courtesy of San Francisco History Center, San Francisco Public Library.)

Police Chief J.B. Martin saw Park Station constructed under his watch in 1910. The station was built despite the strong objection of John McLaren, superintendent of Golden Gate Park, who believed that no building should be constructed within the confines of the park. (Courtesy of San Francisco History Center, San Francisco Public Library.)

Police Chief John F. Seymour (1911), like other chiefs at the turn of the century, had many outstanding recruits from different nations. One of them, Yugoslavian-born Virgil N. Bakulich (SFPD 1894–1919) could write, speak, and read Greek, Russian, Slovenian, Italian, German, and English and is believed to be the most able linguist the department ever had. (Courtesy of San Francisco History Center, San Francisco Public Library.)

Police Chief D.A. White (1911–1920) was knighted and received two orders from King Albert of Belgium, who, on a visit to San Francisco in 1918, took a great liking to the kindly, well-met man. During White's term the SFPD became one of the first police departments in the country to employ women when three "Women Protective Officers" were hired in 1913. (Courtesy of San Francisco History Center, San Francisco Public Library.)

This 1913 image shows the SFPD tug of war team. From left to right are (front row) A. White, an unidentified man (in suit), and P. Phelan; (back row) J. Cameron, Al Schmidt, F.O. Connor, M. Desmonds, and D. Campbell . (Courtesy of San Francisco History Center, San Francisco Public Library.)

Wow! Officer Harry Fisher stops traffic with a babe in arms in this *c*. 1915 image. (Courtesy of San Francisco History Center, San Francisco Public Library.)

A patrolman is pictured with crewmembers of the USS *Jason*, which arrived in San Francisco for the Panama-Pacific International Exposition on April 15, 1915 after a 23,000-mile cruise. It left New York on November 14 with 85 carloads of food, supplies, and Christmas presents for war refugees. After stopping at Austria, Belgium, England, France, Greece, Italy, and Spain to pick up works of art and exposition exhibits, it left Bristol, England, on January 17 for San Francisco. (Courtesy of San Francisco History Center, San Francisco Public Library.)

According to his death notice, patrolman John S. Roche, star 278, was one of the most popular officers in the department. He was born in County Limerick, Ireland, and spent most of his time with the SFPD at Southern Station. Following the 1906 earthquake he was connected with the Potrero Police Station. One of his sons, Thomas, was an officer at Mission Station. He is buried at Holy Cross Cemetery in Colma. (Courtesy of John O'Rourke.)

Shown here are the amazing Maloney brothers who all concurrently served as police officers at the turn of the 20th century. From left to right at the top are Barney Maloney, star 248, sergeant of the San Francisco force; John Maloney, star 394, and Joe Maloney, star 600, both also on the San Francisco force. On the lower left is SFPD officer Edward Maloney, star 146, who was killed in action. At lower right, James George Malone, the oldest of the police brothers, was a member of the Denver traffic squad. George dropped the "y" from his last name, according to family history, after he had to "abruptly leave town." The SFPD also had five generations of continuous police service in California with the Michael Dower family beginning in 1885. The first four generations served in the SFPD while the fifth generation is now with the Burlingame Police Department. (Courtesy of the author.)

This pre-1915 image of three of the five Maloney police brothers and an unknown Maloney include, from left to right, (standing) Bernard Maloney, star 248; Thomas W. Maloney, star 131; and Joseph P. Maloney, star 600; (seated) John E. Maloney, star 394. Thomas Maloney was born in Redwood City in February 1874 and was a blacksmith before he joined the SFPD in 1907. He was charged with neglect of duty by Captain Lemon in 1935, although the judgment board dismissed the charge. He retired in June 1941. Joseph P. Maloney was born in Antioch in 1872 and was a teamster before joining the SFPD in July 1902. He was charged with an illegal arrest by M.J. O'Rourke in November 1904 and the judgment board also dismissed the charge. He died shortly after his retirement in August 1927. John E. Maloney was born in San Jose in April 1863 and was a farmer before he joined the SFPD in 1889. He retired in April 1924. (Courtesy of the author.)

Bernard Maloney, star 248, was born in San Francisco in 1881 and was a watchman before he joined the SFPD in 1904. He made the rank of corporal in April 1914, sergeant in May 1919, and he retired in August 1929. (Courtesy of the author.)

Officer Edward Maloney was shot in the back after wrestling on the ground with his murderer at Sacramento and Davis Streets on April 19, 1915. Firemen A.B. Butterworth and Earl Evans of Engine 12 heard the shots and saw the killer run down the street but lost him after giving chase. Maloney died upon arrival at Harbor Emergency Hospital. Maloney's murderer later told Captain of Detectives Shea, "I cannot remember killing a policeman," and that he "had been drinking heavily." An eyewitness to the tragedy, Herbert H. Blake of 429 Sacramento Street, voluntarily came to police headquarters and picked Russian Anton Staninakis, alias Charles Felker, and his companion Otto Walker out of the lineup as the men who had been halted by Officer Maloney. Staninakis had been captured around 1 a.m. after boarding a ferry for Oakland following a three-hour dragnet over the harbor district. Walker had been captured 30 minutes after the crime at Hilderbrand's saloon at Second and Folsom Streets after bragging how easy it was for someone to kill a policeman and get away with it in the city. Felker and Walker were two of four men who had been involved in a series of holdups in the Barbary Coast. (Courtesy of the author.)

Out of respect, Coroner Leland instructed his deputies not to take the body of Officer Edward Maloney to the morgue. Instead the body was taken from Harbor Emergency Hospital to McBrearty & McCormick undertakers at 915 Valencia Street. Anna Maloney, wife of the slain officer, is seen exiting the funeral parlor praying. "Edward never worried about the dangers of his work. He wouldn't let me think about it," Anna said. "When we were first married, people called on us and told me that my husband was in a very dangerous business. I used to worry about it at first, but Edward wouldn't let me. He'd say that his work wasn't nearly so hazardous as that of many men in other callings. He just didn't know what fear was. If he only had been wounded I'm certain he would have recovered because he was so strong." She also said that she believed the long coat of her husband's uniform had hindered him from reaching his revolver in time to save his life. (Courtesy of the author.)

Officer Maloney was a member of Niantic Parlor No. 105 of the Native Sons of the Golden West. At the time of death he was over 6 feet tall and weighed more than 200 pounds. His police brothers were of similar stature, all over 6 feet and more than 200 pounds. (Courtesy of the author.)

This photograph was taken outside Saint James Church in the Mission District. Officer Maloney had escaped death a year and a half earlier when he disarmed two safe crackers who pointed their guns at him. He was commended by the Police Commission for his bravery. (Courtesy of the author.)

The SFPD pose at Fifteenth and Valencia in 1915. Pacific Coast League ballplayer Art Dikas said he witnessed Babe Ruth hit one out of this ballpark and shatter the window of a residential home. (Courtesy of San Francisco History Center, San Francisco Public Library.)

Commander Theo J. Roche inspects the men and their revolvers in this c. 1915 photo. (Courtesy of San Francisco History Center, San Francisco Public Library.)

President Theodore Roosevelt, visiting San Francisco on Roosevelt Day in 1915, is shown next to an SFPD officer. His cousin, President Franklin Delano Roosevelt, visited San Francisco in September 1938 and informed Chief Quinn that "his force had done the finest policing job he had ever seen outside of the City of New York," and told him to "Tell the boys they had done a good job." (Courtesy of San Francisco History Center, San Francisco Public Library.)

A concert and ball for the Widows and Orphans Aid Association was held at the Civic Auditorium on Monday, February 21, 1916. (Courtesy of the author.)

Police Chief Daniel J. O'Brien (1920–1928) is shown on Boy's Day with "Boy Chief" Donald Bryer. O'Brien personally assisted in the formation of the present-day Federal Bureau of Investigation by contributing 200,000 fingerprints and photographs from the criminal files of the SFPD to the FBI. America's number-one crime nemesis, J. Edgar Hoover, on a visit to San Francisco, stated that "San Francisco is a bright spot on our map. Your Police Department has pushed its drive against organized crime to the point where criminal rackets, as other cities know them, haven't a chance here. Other cities have drives against crime, but not much push." In September 1921, his officers made world news when they arrested silent movie comic Fatty Arbuckle for the murder of Virginia Rappe. Chief O'Brien was also a pioneer in police radio and originally joined the force as a patrolman, star 808. He was responsible for the monthly SFPD magazine *Douglas 2-0*, which began in November 1922. In 1926 he was made president of the International Association of Chiefs at the World Conference in Chicago. He lived his early life south of Market Street and was a brilliant orator. He was laid to rest at Holy Cross Cemetery in Colma. (Courtesy of University of California at Berkeley, Bancroft Library.)

This *c.* 1920 photo shows the SFPD *Patrol* dredging San Francisco Bay. (Courtesy of San Francisco History Center, San Francisco Public Library.)

This photograph, taken in 1920, shows an SFPD review in front of San Francisco City Hall. (Courtesy of San Francisco History Center, San Francisco Public Library.)

This c. 1925 image depicts a motorcycle patrol on parade in the civic center. It was in March of 1925 that the SFPD added chemical warfare capabilities, with tear gas bombs for dispersing mobs, and mustard and other gas bombs for routing out barricaded criminals. (Courtesy of SFPD.)

This image of boxer Jack Dempsey, the world heavyweight champion, star 486, was taken in 1924. Dempsey stated he turned down the job offer of Chief Daniel J. O'Brien, saying, "I'd never make a policeman. It takes too much energy and I'd rather just fool around and do a whole lot of things. I guess I'm restless. Always up to something different. I've been a lot of different things. Now I'm an actor." It's interesting to note that the New York City Police Department made baseball homerun slugger Babe Ruth a lieutenant in the police reserves and gave him a uniform. About this time, Charles McKelvie, better known by his boxing name Chick Devlin, who, with 58 wins and 3 losses narrowly lost his bid for the world's middleweight title, was disqualified from the SFPD after months of stretching exercises and growing mop hair because he was not five foot, nine inches tall. McKelvie went on to serve 39 years in the San Francisco Fire Department. Nowadays even a five-foot male or a four-foot-six female is eligible for police duty. (Courtesy of University of California at Berkeley, Bancroft Library.)

Officer Frank Mascarelli is shown in this 1926 image with Jack O'Keefe. (Courtesy of San Francisco History Center, San Francisco Public Library.)

A Warning to Crooks

"A Warning to Crooks" was the title of this powerful June 1926 cartoon, depicting the police force that was awaiting the "Riff-Raff Element." (Courtesy of San Francisco History Center, San Francisco Public Library.)

An unidentified officer, star 390, poses in a bulletproof vest in this January 1927 image. Currrent technology has made these garments lightweight and very effective against small-arms fire. Today it's mandatory that all SFPD officers wear a bulletproof vest while on duty. (Courtesy of San Francisco History Center, San Francisco Public Library.)

This December 1927 image shows the popular future police chief, William J. Quinn, with Mayor Rolph at the first annual review of the 1,200 juvenile traffic policemen. Rolph gained worldwide fame when he started "Police Day" on February 19, 1927 in the City of San Francisco. Police Chief William J. Quinn (1929–1940) joined the SFPD on November 20, 1906. As chief he completely motorized the department by having radios put in all cars as well as installing a teletype system for inter-department communications. He also founded the Big Brothers Bureau to deal with juveniles. The SFPD Academy opened on October 18, 1937 on the recommendation of Chief Quinn. It was during Quinn's first year as chief that his officers took Ms. Frances Orlando to Bush Street Station, having arrested her for dressing in men's clothes! She told officers she had been wearing pants for four years and was comfortable doing so. (Courtesy of San Francisco History Center, San Francisco Public Library.)

Big James McEachern is shown in September 1928 in full SFPD uniform with the 35-pound weight throw in. This track and field athlete competed in the 1920 Antwerp and 1924 Paris Olympic Games in the hammer throw event. In 1920 in Antwerp he threw the hammer 44.70 meters but did not place in Paris in 1924. He also proudly represented the San Francisco Olympic Club. Years earlier, in 1910, big Joe Walsh, from Bantry, County Cork, Ireland, was considered the largest man ever in the department. Walsh, at 300-plus pounds, was reputed to be "one of the largest Irishmen ever to come out of the Emerald Isle." (Courtesy of San Francisco History Center, San Francisco Public Library.)

Patrolman Eugene Caplis, star 1243, was a member of the Police Flying Squad that was operational day and night. This elite 13-motorcycle squad with sidecars was organized by Sgt. Thomas McInerney. On May 30, 1942, Patrolman Caplis, (the newspaper spelled his name incorrectly as "Caples" on page one), passed away after receiving a blow to the head. The 14-year veteran's widow and 11-year-old daughter were denied Caplis's pension as it was not considered a line-of-duty death. Over the years, other officers experienced similar deaths, or claimed to have acquired deadly viruses on the job, so that now a committee with standards determines what exactly is considered a line-of-duty death. (Courtesy of Lt. Jack Cremen, SFFD.)

This July 1929 image shows a two-officer motorcycle with a sidecar. Notice the tommy gun. The Sidecar Unit was inaugurated by Chief William J. Quinn in 1929 as a mobile reserve that could be assembled in any part of the city within ten minutes. This unit was succeeded by the radio-equipped auto, patrolling the various police districts 24 hours a day and proving to be one of the greatest assets in preventing crime and arresting offenders. (Courtesy of San Francisco History Center, San Francisco Public Library.)

This c. 1929 image shows "speed cop" Walter Mathes with his well-appointed vehicle. (Courtesy of San Francisco History Center, San Francisco Public Library.)

Shown above is the first SFPD firing range at Fort Funston by the Pacific Ocean in the 1920s. Construction of the department's current range, which is located at Lake Merced, was started before World War II and finished during the war by four cops. It opened in 1944. (Courtesy of San Francisco History Center, San Francisco Public Library.)

This photograph shows the police boat *D.A. White*, named after Police Chief David A. White (1911–1920). It was used in April 1943 during the Alcatraz Island prison break. Of the four prisoners who escaped, Harold Brest, a kidnapper and robber, was recaptured after being nicked by a guard's bullet; former Alvin Karpis associate Fred Hunter was caught hiding in a cave; and bank robbers Floyd Hamilton and James Boarman were reported to have drowned. (Courtesy of San Francisco History Center, San Francisco Public Library.)

Sgt. Pat McGee (left) takes a gun from Vincent P. Lynch in this c. 1930 image. (Courtesy of San Francisco History Center, San Francisco Public Library.)

Capt. Arthur Layne was originally from Texas and spent 41 years on the force. While heading up the police academy he made sure officers could type, swim, and take memory tests. Layne was known for leading bold raids in Chinatown. (Courtesy of San Francisco History Center, San Francisco Public Library.)

Two men stand in the line up at the Hall of Justice in the 1930s; the man on the right appears to be a sailor. Years later, in 1962, over $300,000 was pumped into the showroom to add control board that governed the lights to simulate different scenes, such as neon lighting, etc. (Courtesy of San Francisco History Center, San Francisco Public Library.)

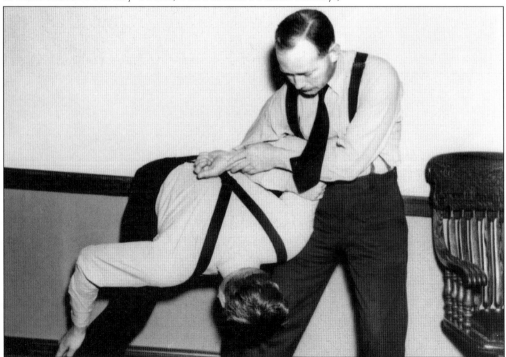

SFPD officers Frank Maskorelli (left) and Arthur O'Keefe practice defense tactics in the 1930s. (Courtesy of San Francisco History Center, San Francisco Public Library.)

Ouch! This *c.* 1930 image shows SFPD officers George McArdle (left) and Herman Webeckeon practicing defense tactics. (Courtesy of San Francisco History Center, San Francisco Public Library.)

SFPD officers sing along with a piano playing Al Jolson in this 1930s image. From left to right are Jerry Argenti, Arthur Garrett, Claude Aradona, Jack Kelly, Ted Andrus, and Claude Aradona. Earlier, in the 1920s, the SFPD jazz band was made famous thanks to the radio, specifically KPO radio. (Courtesy of San Francisco History Center, San Francisco Public Library.)

This October 1930 image shows patrolman A.P. Kerwin (left) with Carl Williams (right). Kerwin was the observant officer who noticed the small taxi driver's hat, which led to Williams's arrest. (Courtesy of San Francisco History Center, San Francisco Public Library.)

This 1931 image shows Officer Carlisle Field with three-and-a-half-year-old Teddy Wolf in an SFPD uniform. "Officer" Wolf is wearing an SFPD surgeon badge. Smart kid! Years later, on June 14, 2000, Police Chief Fred Lau swore in five-year-old Eric Watson who had one overriding desire: to be a San Francisco police officer. While the department has an age minimum recruiting requirement, it was waived this one time for Eric, who had been diagnosed with Wilm's Tumor. The Police Department, in conjunction with the Greater Make-a-Wish Foundation, decided that Eric's wish was to be fulfilled, and he was officially made part of the 195th recruit class. (Courtesy of San Francisco History Center, San Francisco Public Library.)

The July 1933 image above shows police engaged in the then-common practice of throwing confiscated guns into the San Francisco Bay. (Courtesy of San Francisco History Center, San Francisco Public Library.)

In June 1934 robbers attempted to steal a 300-pound safe from the fifth floor of an office building but fled when they realized the SFPD was on to the job. Officers shown are Bill Guthrie (left) and Don Willetts. Clem De Amicis shines his flashlight from a higher perch. (Courtesy of San Francisco History Center, San Francisco Public Library.)

Police raid a Communist bookstore at 121 Haight Street in July 1934. (Courtesy of San Francisco History Center, San Francisco Public Library.)

This July 1934 image shows two police officers chasing a man during the 1934 longshoremen's strike. On July 5, 1934 blood ran in the streets of San Francisco as 1,000 embattled policemen held at bay 5,000 longshoremen and their sympathizers in a sweeping front south of Market Street and east of Second Street. The city's hospitals were filled with the wounded and gassed. By midnight tanks were rolling along the Embarcadero, helmeted soldiers had fixed bayonets, and machine guns had been placed on some buildings. (Courtesy of San Francisco History Center, San Francisco Public Library.)

This July 1934 image shows "Bloody Thursday," when Howard Sperry and Gene Olson were shot by police on Mission Street during the longshoremen's strike. Two men died during the strike: longshoreman Howard Sperry on Mission at Stuart Street, seen here, and another man around the corner, a Greek Communist cook named Nick Counderakais, who called himself Bordoise, and had been working in the International Longshoremen's Association relief kitchen. (Courtesy of San Francisco History Center, San Francisco Public Library.)

During the longshoremen's strike of 1934 the SFPD was assisted by the California National Guard called out by Governor Merriam. Printed in one of the California newspapers in July 1934 were the verbal instructions Lt. Col. David P. Hardy gave his 159th Infantry troops and the 125th Coast Artillery before they left their armory: "If it is a question of you or the rioters, get them first. If you are attacked clip them, then bayonet them, then use bullets." On July 31, ship owners agreed to settle by arbitration and Harry Bridges, head of the International Longshoremen's Association, sent his men back to work. (Quote courtesy of California Military Museum archives, Sacramento; photo courtesy of the author.)

This October 1934 image shows two police officers drawing their guns in a joking response to a mural painted on the 212-foot-tall Coit Tower on Telegraph Hill depicting a crime in progress. (Courtesy San Francisco History Center, San Francisco Public Library.)

This October 1935 photo shows Officer Dan McSweeney and his horse, Comanche, who McSweeney exercised regularly in the bay off Hunters Point. McSweeney's goal was to have the two-and-a-half-year-old stallion be the first horse to swim the Golden Gate. That honor actually went to a horse named Blackie. (Courtesy of San Francisco History Center, San Francisco Public Library.)

This January 1936 image shows, from left to right, San Francisco Mayor Angelo Rossi, U.S. Attorney General Homer S. Cummings, Warden James A. Johnston, and SFPD Chief William J. Quinn inspecting cells on Alcatraz Island Federal Penitentiary. (Courtesy of San Francisco History Center, San Francisco Public Library.)

This 1937 lesson in fingerprinting was given by Inspector Francis X. Latulipe to rookie officer Robert Seyden. (Courtesy of San Francisco History Center, San Francisco Public Library.)

Officer Gus Wuth is surrounded by an army of happy kids in this June 1937 photo. A few weeks earlier, the officer had been shifted from Redding Elementary School to Franklin School. The kids sent a petition to Chief Quinn that they wanted back their "favorite policeman," who was their friend, adviser, baseball umpire, and arbitrator. After this event, the students at Franklin School drew up a petition to demand the return of their patrolman, Tom Hurly. (Courtesy of San Francisco History Center, San Francisco Public Library.)

This August 1937 image shows the SFPD's latest weapon in its fight against crime, "mechanical brains" being operated by Mrs. Eleanor Brooks (left) and Ms. Virginia McCarthy. To operate the mechanical brains, the cards were first punched with holes, then sorted by the machine, and when two cards were shown to have a similar record, that individual could possibly be linked to a crime. The third machine (unattended) made an analysis of the facts. (Courtesy of San Francisco History Center, San Francisco Public Library.)

This September 1937 photograph shows two unidentified men practicing defense tactics. That same year, the SFPD moved gold stored at the old mint to the new mint. According to a letter to Chief Quinn, "There were 1,288 truck loads of a total weight of 12,839,578 tons involved." During the move no precious metals were lost. (Courtesy of San Francisco History Center, San Francisco Public Library.)

The first SFPD Police Academy was established in October 1937 and the first class graduated in January 1938. The academy was at Thirty-seventh Avenue and Fulton Street. From left to right are (front row) Sgt. George B. Duncan II; Captain Skelley; Chief William J. Quinn; Officer Tom Collins; Capt. Arthur B. Layne, who will be remembered for founding the academy and his raids on Chinese gambling establishments; and retired criminologist Lt. Frank Latulip; (middle row) newly appointed recruits Thomas W. Cassidy, William Vallentine, Arnold Schaffer, and Ray Seyden; (back row) Niles Driver Jr., Frank Thornly, Gus Palmeri, Hazelton French, Jim Donahu, and Gil Dowd. The academy later moved to the fifth floor of the Hall of Justice, Treasure Island, Silver Avenue, and then to its current location at Diamond Heights. The academy taught physical education and yawara, a martial art. Jitsuzo Ishidu taught yawara to the SFPD and FBI and was the only yawara instructor in the United States. (Courtesy of San Francisco History Center, San Francisco Public Library.)

These three boys from Los Angeles who ran away to take a firsthand look at the newly opened Golden Gate Bridge in November 1937 included, from left to right, Gerald O'Shea, James Robinson, and Dewey Adams. Officers Ed Miskal (left) and Harold Brown, shown behind the adventurous boys, provided the tour. (Courtesy of San Francisco History Center, San Francisco Public Library.)

This December 1937 image shows, from left to right, Bill Herman, George Badger (with "dragnet"), and Rudy Kopfu. This was long before the TV show *Dragnet* and before the SFPD actually had an officer named Jack Webb in the 1950s. (Courtesy of San Francisco History Center, San Francisco Public Library.)

Lotus Liu and Slater Barkentine are shown double-parking their rickshaw in January 1938 on a downtown street, while Officer Bob Martin gives them a ticket. (Courtesy of San Francisco History Center, San Francisco Public Library.)

This February 1938 image of Southern Police Station shows the physical beauty of its exterior. Today several modern stations boast works of arts both inside and out and are worth a visit by the public. (Courtesy of San Francisco History Center, San Francisco Public Library.)

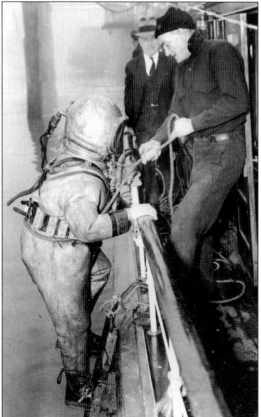

Police diver Bill Wood searches for a body at Pier 14 in 1938. The other men pictured are Bill Ahern (with hat) and Jack Hale (with phone). (Courtesy of San Francisco History Center, San Francisco Public Library.)

This *c.* 1939 photo shows motorcycle officer Herbert M. Brandt at the World's Fair Expo toll gate giving this motorist a ticket. The driver, Herman W. Littrell, exclaimed, "You can't tag a washtub, officer!" This one had two hand pedals, two washtubs, and four wheels and was dubbed the "Jitterbug Special." Littrell drove this contraption 2,500 miles from Elm Springs, Arkansas, to the Golden Gate International Exposition. (Courtesy of San Francisco History Center, San Francisco Public Library.)

This October 1940 photo shows Officer Harold Richardson with Thomas Weal, 21, of Chicago, who was being held for investigation. The officer had noticed the shabbily dressed man with a new suitcase full of $1,200 worth of jewelry, including 11 ladies' wristwatches, 5 men's wristwatches, 2 pocket watches, 8 cameo rings, 14 signet rings and 12 assorted other rings. (Courtesy of San Francisco History Center, San Francisco Public Library.)

Police Chief Charles W. Dullea (1940–1947) was appointed by Mayor Rossi just prior to World War II. Dullea, a former U.S. Marine who was considered a policeman's chief because he had risen through the ranks, ran the department like a military organization. During this time over half of the force—more than 400 men—served in the war. Because of this, the auxiliary police force was established with 4-Fs and grandfathers for traffic details so that the rest of the force could focus on other tasks, such as taking up preassigned locations during air raid drills. (Courtesy of San Francisco History Center, San Francisco Public Library.)

These new police cars, shown outside the civic auditorium on Grove Street in April 1941, included 26 Ford V-8 automobiles. Delivery was made by Babe Maggini of Maggini Motor Car Company to SFPD Police Chief Charles Dullea. (Courtesy of San Francisco History Center, San Francisco Public Library.)

Officer Richard J. Hanley was dubbed "the perfect policeman" by former Mayor James Rolph. Hanley was never late for reporting because he used two alarm clocks to get up every day at 2:30 p.m. In an unusual coincidence he passed away at 2:30 p.m. one afternoon in March 1941. Despite his tough, 35-year beat in Butchertown, he was never called on the carpet for anything but commendation, never missed a day's work, was never late, and never used a day of sick leave. (Courtesy of San Francisco History Center, San Francisco Public Library.)

Joe Gremminger oversaw the SFPD's arsenal in the 1940s. Here he looks over a tommy gun. The collection also included rifles, machine guns, revolvers, and tear gas throwers. (Courtesy of San Francisco History Center, San Francisco Public Library.)

The crew of the World War II B-24 Liberator *Holm's Rocket* at March Field included future SFPD Officer John Barisone (bottom row, left), who later became one of the lead investigators in the Golden Dragon Restaurant Massacre in 1977. During the war the SFPD worked long hours to make up for the loss of 400 members who entered the armed forces, and the military provided several future recruits who were well trained. (Courtesy of the Barisone family.)

Chinese Americans served in the SFPD well before Herbert P. Lee, who was thought to be the first, in 1957. A significant discovery in the archives shows that during World War II, a Chinese American was made a member of the SFPD Auxiliary along with an African American, as pictured on the following page. Shown here in March 1942 looking down the sight of a police shotgun are William O'Brien (left) and B. Chung. (Courtesy of San Francisco History Center, San Francisco Public Library.)

This 1942 image shows Officer Fred Franke giving a lecture with B. Chung in the front row and, three seats behind him, an African-American member of the SFPD Auxiliary. This photo is compelling as it shows three races of people all sitting together in one learning environment, demonstrating that the SFPD was truly progressive. (Courtesy of San Francisco History Center, San Francisco Public Library.)

Here a Japanese two-man sub is paraded through Chinatown under the watchful eyes of the SFPD in 1942. Captured during the Japanese attack on Pearl Harbor, it was used on the mainland in a war bonds campaign tour. Priest Henry Yee performed ancient Chinese rituals to rid the evil from the craft, dubbed "Tojo's Cigar." In addition, numerous firecrackers were thrown at the sub. (Courtesy of San Francisco History Center, San Francisco Public Library.)

Inspector Jack Manion, who retired in 1946, was known as the Chinatown police chief. He was credited with ending the tong wars that bloodied the streets of Chinatown for 50 years. He told the six powerful tongs, or Chinese secret societies, there would be no more opium, slave girls, or killing. Manion was nicknamed "mau yee," the Chinese word for "cat." One tong that was forced out of business described him as having "two eyes in front, one eye behind, and never sleeps." Manion died in 1959. (Courtesy of San Francisco History Center, San Francisco Public Library.)

This May 1947 photo shows Admiral Baron Ahab von Muller being placed in the "paddy wagon," after illegally feeding the pigeons at Civic Center Plaza. The vehicle is now called a patrol wagon. (Courtesy of San Francisco History Center, San Francisco Public Library.)

This July 1947 photo shows Police Officer Walter Christensen at his retirement event at the San Francisco Zoological Gardens. He received a gold star from Officer Tom Price and a fishing reel from his buddies at the zoo. Christensen had been a patrolman at the zoo since it was established at this location in 1929 and saw the Works Progress Administration build a large part of the facility during the Great Depression. (Courtesy of San Francisco History Center, San Francisco Public Library.)

Police Chief Michael Riordan (1947) was a deputy chief during World War II and organized the auxiliary police force. An Irishman from County Kerry who grew up in the neighborhood of the famous Killarney Lakes, he arrived in America in 1907 and entered SFPD service on March 31, 1913. (Courtesy of San Francisco History Center, San Francisco Public Library.)

This April 1948 image shows a drinking fountain dedicated to the memory of Schultz, the first dog to be a regular member of the SFPD. Sgt. Anthony Kane points to the inscription, which refers to Schultz's death, by poison, a few months earlier: "To the memory of a dog; drink to the memory of Schultz today, his friendliness to man did him betray." When the dog was a victim of a hit and run in 1945 he was given a star engraved "Schultz—Golden Gate Park—Police Station." (Courtesy of San Francisco History Center, San Francisco Public Library.)

Police Chief Michael Mitchell (1948–1950) was appointed to the department on January 1, 1908 and made chief on January 13, 1948. For years before he became chief he rode what was known in the department as the "night prowl car." This car became famous for the number of criminals its crew brought in. In 1945, he was chosen by his former partner Chief Charles Dullea to head the select 70-man security company that ensured the safety of the international delegates and President Harry S. Truman at the first meeting of the United Nations in San Francisco. His able leadership in the effort helped prompt his selection as chief. (Courtesy of Karen Mitchell-Hanning.)

This undated image shows a young Mike Mitchell relaxing with friends and a bottle of wine. From left to right are Louis Castagnetto, Officer Tom Mitchell (brother of Mike), future SFPD chief Mike Mitchell (with star), and George Curran, a neighbor who appears to be in a dress. (Courtesy of Karen Mitchell-Hanning.)

This January 1949 photograph of youngsters from the Sunset District shows, from left to right, Gunard Mahl, Phil Mc Millen, and Dan Augustiny skating on Lake Mallard in Golden Gate Park. Four policemen were on hand to tell the kids this activity was very dangerous due to thin ice and that they must stop skating. (Courtesy of San Francisco History Center, San Francisco Public Library.)

In July 1949 Police Chief Michael Mitchell greeted eight new SFPD policewomen who had graduated from the academy. Women first entered the department as Woman Protective Officers around the turn of the century and were initially matrons. Shown here are, from left to right, Chief Mitchell, Genevieve Bayreuther, Mary Loftus, Virginia Cullen, Claire Lutz, Shirley Schroff, Margaret Spraggins, Margaret Dolan, and Dorothy Boughton. Schroff later married SFPD Police Officer John Barisone, making them the first married couple in the SFPD. Today there are several. (Courtesy of Shirley Barisone.)

This October 1949 image shows just one of the violent murder scenes that SFPD officers are regularly exposed to in the performance of their duty. The victims, Robert Savage and Mrs. Margery R. Wilson, were slain in a drugstore robbery. The store's safe was cleaned out by the robber(s) who had no regard whatsoever for human life. (Courtesy of San Francisco History Center, San Francisco Public Library.)

Three

1951–PRESENT

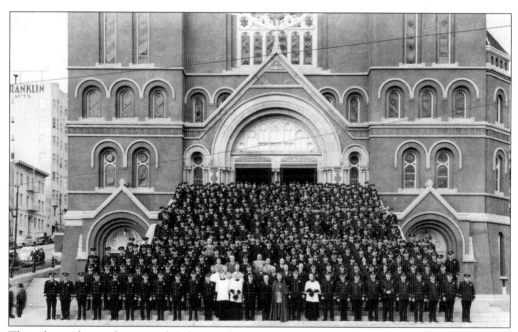

This photo shows the annual Police and Fire Mass at Saint Mary's Cathedral on Van Ness Avenue in 1950. This second St. Mary's Cathedral was built on Van Ness Avenue in 1891, but the structure was destroyed by fire in 1962. The first St. Mary's, built in 1854, is located on California Street at Grant Avenue. The current Cathedral of Saint Mary of the Assumption, known familiarly as St. Mary's Cathedral, has become a landmark that annually draws thousands of people. The building was completed in 1970. The new cathedral, which combines the rich traditions of the Catholic faith with modern technology, was formally blessed on May 5, 1971. Pope John Paul II celebrated Mass at St. Mary's Cathedral during his visit to San Francisco in 1987. Many SFPD and SFFD funerals are held at that location. (Courtesy of the Barisone family.)

Snippy the police horse is shown at Argonne School with policeman Emmett Hanley on Snippy's last day of duty in March 1950. The 18-year-old horse was known to stop by the school daily and give the youngsters free rides to the corner and back. Note the handsome ribbon on Snippy's bridle. (Courtesy of San Francisco History Center, San Francisco Public Library.)

This June 1950 image shows Patrolman Brian McDonnell, star 173, with two-year-old Linda Durand at Park Police Station as she tries on a real policeman's star. Linda was found wandering around Haight and Clayton Streets and was later picked up by her thankful mother. (Courtesy of San Francisco History Center, San Francisco Public Library.)

Criminologist Frank La Tulipe is shown in this July 1950 image in the crime lab at the Hall of Justice. At right in this picture is a ballistics comparison microscope that tells experts what gun a bullet is fired from. Other devices shown are used for magnifying and evaluating evidence. Over $100,000 was spent to make this lab state of the art. (Courtesy of San Francisco History Center, San Francisco Public Library.)

In July 1950, Leonard F. Wiebe, a police technician, demonstrated a simple test to spotlight the slightest trace of human blood. A drop of a mixture of hydrogen peroxide, acetic acid, and benzidine produces a blue stain on the rag. (Courtesy of San Francisco History Center, San Francisco Public Library.)

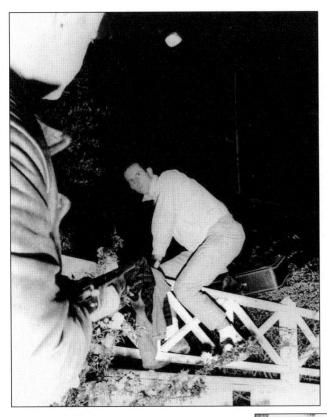

This *c.* 1950 image shows that crime does not pay. The SFPD officer in this night scene shot has his rifle pointed at the suspect, who has some real explaining to do. The suspect is climbing over a fence in the middle of the night with a suitcase and wearing gloves. (Courtesy of San Francisco History Center, San Francisco Public Library.)

From left to right are police officers Mary Loftus, Claire Lutz, and Shirley Schroff in the Sunset District in the 1950s. Their uniforms were tailored after those worn by the WAVES in World War II, with a blue twill jacket and matching skirt. Female officers also wore white shirts and gloves, and a beret with insignia in front. A black tie and black pumps completed the outfit. A shoulder strap bag was issued for toting guns and handcuffs. These dresses were redesigned from an earlier version created by I. Magnin and Company in the 1940s. In 1944 Officer Doris Chapman, star 507, arrested a jaywalker who called her uniform a "monkey suit." Judge Cronin fined the man ten times the normal amount for his rude remark. Duties for women officers included cases of all boys and girls under 18, watching public dance halls, working with broken homes, abortion cases, and events where people gathered. They earned the same pay as men. (Courtesy of Shirley Barisone.)

In this June 1950 photograph, Officers Paul Never (left) and Ford Long pull guard duty at the DeYoung Museum in Gold Gate park. They are sitting on approximately $40 million worth of Austrian art that was sent to the museum from the Vienna Museum's collection of masterpieces. (Courtesy of San Francisco History Center, San Francisco Public Library.)

Police Chief Michael Gaffey (1951–1955) disbanded the super vice squad on April 18, 1954, claiming that prostitution, gambling, and bookmaking were at an "irreducible minimum." Gaffey stated that except for mop-up operations on miscellaneous vice and gambling arrests made by the squad, its four members would return to their regular assignments with the Bureau of Inspectors. (Courtesy of San Francisco History Center, San Francisco Public Library.)

Pictured here are Inspector James Fales and stenographer Dorothy Murphy of the Missing Persons Bureau in 1951. They were looking for Dolores Zimmerman, daughter of a Presidio army officer. Years later, on February 10, 1984, the disappearance of 10-year-old Kevin Collins at Oak and Masonic Streets while he waited for the No. 43 bus, made national headlines, including the front cover of *Time* magazine. (Courtesy of San Francisco History Center, San Francisco Public Library.)

A solo cop on a motorcycle, Officer Anthony Troche is pictured in June 1951 in the Mission District with suspect Fred Bales and two boys, 12-year-old Floyd Burdette (pointing) and 13-year-old Gerald Felix. The boys had chased three holdup men who took $2,200 and informed the officer, "Get them! It's a holdup!" One of the three robbers was immediately caught. (Courtesy of San Francisco History Center, San Francisco Public Library.)

Officers John McQuaide (left) and James Cannon are shown at the home distillery of Albert Liberati Bruno at 67 Valparaiso in August 1951. This illegal operation was brought to light via an explosion and fire; Bruno had lit a cigarette and set off alcohol fumes from the illicit still. (Courtesy of San Francisco History Center, San Francisco Public Library.)

Taken at Camp Roberts, this May 1952 cover image of the *San Francisco Police and Peace Officers' Journal* shows members of the 347th Military Police Detachment, from left to right, Sgts. Thomas Guzzetti, Bert Everding, Glen Johnson, George F. Lockhart, Ralph C. McKinley, Peter C. Zelis, and Robert L. Schoenstein, all SFPD officers. Incidentally, the post was named for a World War I U.S. Army solider, Corporal Roberts, a San Franciscan, who in France allowed his partner to exit a sinking tank first, knowing he would drown. Officer Thomas Guzzetti died in a Sutter Street bar shootout in the line of duty on January 1, 1954. He was hit three times, once by an SFPD "friendly fire" bullet that may have been the fatal shot, according to the autopsy report. (Courtesy of San Francisco History Center, San Francisco Public Library.)

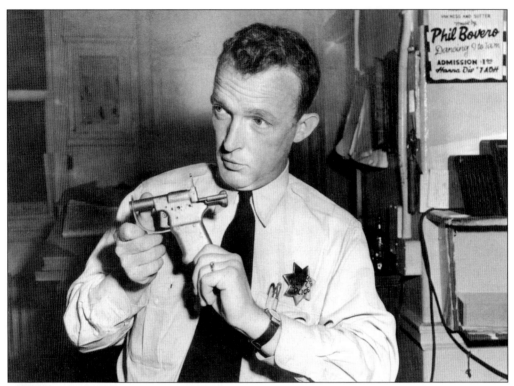

Officer William McDonald appears in this 1952 image with a homemade .45 slug gun. (Courtesy of San Francisco History Center, San Francisco Public Library.)

Patrolman Joseph Albrecht is decked out in his issued foul weather gear in November 1953 at the point where Stockton Street, Ellis Street, and Market Street converge. (Courtesy of San Francisco History Center, San Francisco Public Library.)

This June 1954 image shows "hero cops" Frank Gannon (left) and Wayne Kirby. At 3 a.m. both officers became aware of fumes from an apartment house's broken refrigeration unit at 345 Jones Street and ran through the first three levels alerting people. Then, putting cloths over their faces, the men went up to the fourth and fifth floors to do the same. They were credited with saving 55 lives. (Courtesy of San Francisco History Center, San Francisco Public Library)

Policeman George Clement of Richmond Station holds a piece of ornamentation broken off a post in the Japanese Tea Garden in August 1954. (Courtesy of San Francisco History Center, San Francisco Public Library.)

Officer George Anderson walks with Michael Patrick Collins on Diamond at Bosworth Street in this c. 1955 image. (Courtesy of San Francisco History Center, San Francisco Public Library.)

Police Chief George Healy (1955–1956) is sworn in as the chief of police. (Courtesy of San Francisco History Center, San Francisco Public Library.)

This January 1955 photograph shows SFPD officers frisking suspect Jack Young after locating him in the trunk of a garaged car. The newspaper caption read, "This could be the loot." From left to right are Lt. John Curran, Officer James Van Pelt, Jack Young, Officer Dick Wader, and Vic Giannini. (Courtesy of San Francisco History Center, San Francisco Public Library.)

This February 1955 photograph shows Bud Abbott and Lou Costello at the automobile show at the civic auditorium, helping to increase ticket sales to the Policeman's Ball. Abbott (on left) is shown with Officer Henry Pengel, Costello, and Policewoman Margaret Dillon, who warded off Costello's affections. (Courtesy of San Francisco History Center, San Francisco Public Library.)

This April 1955 image shows members of the crime lab, including, from left to right, John Lucien Barisone, star 982; Walt Ihle; unidentified; Harry Merrill; unidentified; and Reno Rapagnani. Duties of the crime lab included visiting crime scenes and searching for evidence, fingerprinting, assisting victims, testifying in court, and drawing sketches of the crime scene. (Courtesy of the Barisone family.)

The funeral at Saint Peter's for motorcycle officer Gordon Olivera, who died as a result of an accident with an automobile on Anza Street, took place in 1955. Olivera was not wearing a helmet and it was believed that if he had been, he might have survived the accident. Pallbearers in this photo are John Kellejian, Al Aguilar, and Paul McConnell (on left); and J. McKiernan, Tom Walsh, and Dick Armeit (on right). (Courtesy of San Francisco History Center, San Francisco Public Library.)

Police Chief Frank Ahern (1956–1958), born in 1900 south of Market Street of Italian and Irish ancestry, turned the department upside down and "brought back esprit de corps." Ahern fought for better tools for his officers and spent months bringing the arsonist from the tragic New Amsterdam Hotel fire to justice. While he was raiding two notorious abortion rings, he was urged by an implicated woman to help himself to the $280,000 in cash from her safe, but Ahern had her arrested and added the charge of attempted bribery. He was also detailed to the FBI and worked in New York during that detail. Ahern died of a heart attack while enjoying a Labor Day baseball game at Seals Stadium in 1958 and was laid to rest at Holy Cross Cemetery in Colma. (Courtesy of San Francisco History Center, San Francisco Public Library.)

Officer Charles McLaughlin is pictured here with a two-and-a-half-year-old boy at Mission Station in August 1956. The boy told the officer his name was Mike but it proved to be Mark. Two and a half hours later the frantic parents caught up with him. (Courtesy of San Francisco History Center, San Francisco Public Library.)

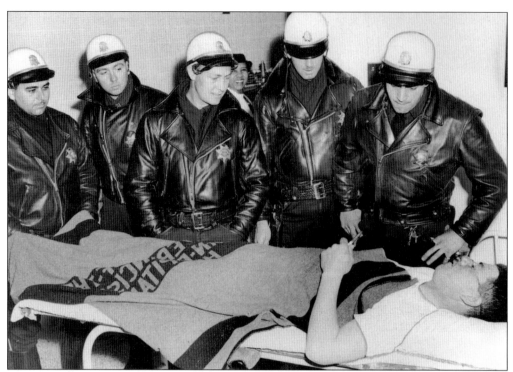

This May 1957 photo shows motorcycle officer Paul Robinson at Mission Emergency Hospital after he was injured by a car at Columbus and Broadway. His crash helmet was credited with saving the 35-year-old officer's life when the driver of the car ran a red light and hit him. (Courtesy of San Francisco History Center, San Francisco Public Library.)

Officer Ed Cantwell of the Mounted Unit gives young Kenneth Kristensen the once-over as he observes the child with a large firecracker on the Fourth of July 1957. Not to worry: that's only a box of candy the horse appears to be interested in. (Courtesy of San Francisco History Center, San Francisco Public Library.)

In August 1957 this five-year-old lost boy was found wandering the streets and was taken to Northern Station. Officer Ray Yazzalino (left) and Officer John Monsen, star 289, allowed the boy to answer police telephones. The boy could not give officers his own name; instead, he gave some 20 different ones. (Courtesy of San Francisco History Center, San Francisco Public Library.)

This September 1957 image shows two officers at Taraval Police Station who caught an ex-con with a bag of barbiturates. Officers Gus Despotakis (left) and Lloyd Crosby count the bottles of illegal drugs. (Courtesy of San Francisco History Center, San Francisco Public Library.)

In October 1957 Herbert P. Lee was sworn in as the first Chinese regular member of the SFPD. Prior to joining the force, Lee worked as a service station attendant while attending San Francisco State College. He had a wife and a daughter named Penny. The news article about the event read "Integration Landmark First Chinese Joins SF Police Force." He was given the Chinatown beat. (Although Lee is cited as the first Chinese SFPD officer, there are references to Chinese serving in the SFPD Auxiliary in the early 1940s.) (Courtesy of San Francisco History Center, San Francisco Public Library.)

Mounted patrolman Charley Conrad ties the shoelaces of Patricia Scalione, a first grader at Lafayette School, in November 1957 at Thirty-seventh and Balboa. Officer Conrad was at the intersection each morning and afternoon to escort his pals across the street, and they often would report to him when they lost a tooth or did not like a homework assignment. (Courtesy of San Francisco History Center, San Francisco Public Library.)

This *c.* 1958 image shows police trying to control unruly fans during a football game at Kezar Stadium. A fence was later installed at the east end of the bowl to keep the general admission patrons from drifting into the more expensive reserve seats, which helped crowd control. (Courtesy of San Francisco History Center, San Francisco Public Library.)

Police Chief Thomas J. Cahill (1958–1970) was well respected, and the current Hall of Justice was named in his honor in March 1994. In 1958 the San Francisco Police Department was confronted with the growing problem of juvenile delinquency, and to counteract this trend, the Police Athletic League (PAL) was established in 1959. Cahill was actually fired by then Mayor Joseph Alioto while on his honeymoon with his second wife. It was also during Cahill's time as chief in 1968 that a veteran officer, calling himself "Sgt. Sunshine," smoked a joint on the steps of city hall to protest marijuana laws. He was arrested and fired. (Courtesy of San Francisco History Center, San Francisco Public Library.)

This photo shows a scale model of the current Thomas J. Cahill Hall of Justice, which was built as a direct result of the successful bond issue of 1956. Notice the helicopter landing zone on top; the other landing area for SFPD aerial assets was at Crissy Field in the Presidio. The two upper floors of the facility house the city jail, in addition to a San Bruno detention facility. Below the six floor are administrative offices, courtrooms, and chambers. The Memorial Wall, which is open daily to the public, is on the ground floor of this facility. (Courtesy of San Francisco History Center, San Francisco Public Library.)

The former Hall of Justice, built after the 1906 earthquake and fire and located on Kearny and Washington Streets across from Porthsmouth Square, is shown here in 1961 before it was demolished. Some officers referred to this property as the "old girl." The SFPD's telephone number at this juncture was SUTTER 1-2020. (Courtesy of San Francisco History Center, San Francisco Public Library.)

This March 1960 image shows the SFPD Underwater Rescue Unit. This skin diver, or "frogman," platoon was formed to hunt for submerged weapons, bodies, or criminal evidence. This unit, which often practiced at Aquatic Park, consisted of Ray Anderson, Paul Schneider, Richard Moore, Sgt. Gene Messerschmidt, and Donald Cavanaugh. (Courtesy of San Francisco History Center, San Francisco Public Library.)

This c. 1960 image shows an officer's silhouette as he uses a blue police call box. These boxes operated before telephones came into use and have saved many police officers' lives. Initially the boxes contained a tapper that an officer would tap in order to activate a signal in the station that all was well. If an officer failed to tap in, a sergeant would dispatch someone to check on him. As telephones became more common they were installed in these same boxes. To hang up the phone the policeman had to slam the door of the box. When sworn in, a new police officer would get a star and a key to the call box. The early keys were bronze and five inches long while today they are the size of a house key. (Courtesy of San Francisco History Center, San Francisco Public Library.)

This June 1960 image shows SFPD Officer William "Bill" Stathes posing in front of the Golden Gate Bridge. Stathes was the Iron Man winner in 1958, and placed fourth in the 1960 Mr. America contest, sixth in 1961, and seventh in 1962. In addition, he took third in the Mr. Pacific Coast contest in 1959 and fifth in 1961. He also made the following magazine covers: *Ironman* in February 1960 and December 1962, and *Strength and Health* in August 1961. He pumped his muscles up daily at the Central YMCA at Leavenworth and Golden Gate Avenue. Stathes was also made famous in 1962 for catching kidnappers. (Courtesy of San Francisco History Center, San Francisco Public Library.)

This is the August 1961 cover of *Strength & Health* magazine featuring SFPD policeman William "Bill" Stathes with Lana Greene. Bill loved outdoor training at the first "Muscle Beach," which was operated by fellow policeman Lt. Tom Carey, star 1615 (SFPD 1954–1979). (Courtesy of Jim Schmitz.)

This touching September 1961 photo shows the true teamwork of a father and daughter in action. Policeman Charles Myer and his 11-year-old daughter, Claire, direct traffic at a school crossing. (Courtesy of San Francisco History Center, San Francisco Public Library.)

This ticket stub comes from the 13th annual baseball game between the San Francisco Policemen and the San Francisco Firemen at Candlestick Park on Monday afternoon, July 4, 1960. Admission was $1 and children under 12 years old were admitted free. Proceeds benefitted the needy children of San Francisco. (Courtesy of San Francisco History Center, San Francisco Public Library.)

Motorcycle policeman Robert Mattox, star 695, is pictured in September 1961 with a switchblade he found on a suspect after capturing him in a trailer unit. Joe Borg and his wife, Mary, had earlier been robbed at the Fairfax Grocery at Fairfax Avenue and Hunters Point. (Courtesy of San Francisco History Center, San Francisco Public Library.)

The Dog Patrol Unit was established in May 1962 by Police Chief Tom Cahill. The seven members of the first Dog Patrol Unit, known as the "Magnificent Seven," were, from left to right, Sgt. Gus Bruneman and Tonka; Lt. Jerry D'Arcy and Ohren; Lt. Walter Brauschweig and Wotan; Bob McDonald and Sultan; Sgt. Mario Tovani and Nemo; Lt. Ken Foss and Thor; and Lt. Art O'Keefe and Rome. There were six German shepherds and one Doberman Pinscher. The first dog to die in the line of duty was Sultan from a 50-foot drop at the Golden Gate Bridge in September 1963. Many dogs did not make this elite unit due to gun shyness, unstable temperament, or physical defects. One of the first assignments was Halloween 1962, when two dogs routed a mob of 500 bottle-throwing pranksters on Fillmore Street. Sergeant Bruneman said, "They did the work of 50 officers." The seven police officers were given training gear, aluminum dog dishes, a book on raising German shepherds, and an introductory lecture by a World War II dog training expert for the German army, Heinz Peters. A single word commanded the dog to attack while a closely guarded word called off the attack. (Courtesy of San Francisco History Center, San Francisco Public Library.)

In 1962 Patrol Special SFPD Officer John J. Candido, shown here with a .357 Smith and Wesson magnum, survived a bullet shot directly into the back of his head by a robber with a U.S. Army Colt automatic .45. Before he passed out in the hospital, Candido claimed he saw a bright light and then a vision of the Virgin Mary putting her arms around him and embracing him. Dr. Edmund J. Morrissey removed the bullet and saved him. Known as a consummate cop, Candido served as a U.S. marshal, an ambulance driver, and a sheriff, and worked for the coroner, as well as being made an honorary fireman when he arrested arsonists who were creating havoc in the city. He even provided security protection to the Swedish consulate. He arrested rapists, armed robbers, and cat burglars. He is most well known for cleaning up two drug-infested single-resident occupancy hotels: the Broadway Hotel at Polk and Broadway and the Burbank Hotel at Leavenworth and Turk. (Courtesy of the Candido family.)

This SFPD shield-shaped patch was worn on both sleeves. The Spanish "Oro en Paz, Fierro en Guerra," means "Gold in Peace, Iron in War." The upper portion of this patch reads "Patrol Special," identifying a police officer per 830.1 of the California State penal code. Other components of the SFPD have similar shields, such as the SFPD Reserve's patch, which on the upper portion of the patch states "Reserve." The Patrol Special Police Officers were paid by property owners, storekeepers, and people living in the neighborhoods they patrolled for their livelihood and not through the City of San Francisco's payroll. (Courtesy of the Candido family.)

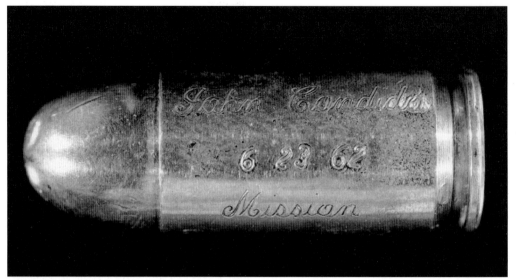

This bullet really did have Officer Candido's name on it. After being taken out of his head in surgery it was reattached to the casing and engraved with his name and the date and location of the shooting. Gunman Vernon Haggard entered Grayson's Clothing Store at 2630 Mission Street, pointed a .45 at the store manager, and said, "I'm not fooling around. I want every cent you've got in the place." He got $500 and ran off with his getaway man, Melvin Herman Fehr, both Folsom Prison alums. Officer Candido approached Fehr, took his German Lugar 9 mm gun away, and then confronted Haggard outside the entrance. Candido managed to get off three shots, but fell when Haggard got him above the right ear, at the base of his skull, with this bullet. (Courtesy of the Candido family.)

This is star 2621, which belonged to Patrol Special SFPD Officer John Candido. The Patrol Special Police have the six-pointed Star of David, while the SFPD regulars have a seven-pointed star. Initially in San Francisco, Special Police worked in banks and wore green uniforms. They were later among the first SFPD officers to wear the famous blue uniform. Founded in 1847, the organization started two full years before the SFPD regulars. (Courtesy of the Candido family.)

Patrol Special SFPD Officer John Candido received the First Grade Meritorious Certificate and later the Gold Medal of Valor. In July 1970 Chief Al Nelder instituted this one-and-a-half-inch, circular valor medal, which was designed by patrolman Tom Mulkeen in two days. Nelder stated:

For men ready to give up their lives, or be injured in going up against a gun or a knife, a medal is the least we can honor them with. It's the highest award for valor merited when the following elements exist: Outstanding bravery above and beyond that expected in the line of duty. Where failure to take such action would not justify censure. Where risk of life actually existed and the officer had sufficient time to evaluate that risk. Where the objective is of sufficient importance to justify the risk. Where the officer accomplished the objective or was prevented from accomplishing the objective by incurring a disabling injury or death.

This valor medal can be worn on an officer's uniform only on ceremonial occasions. (Courtesy of the Candido family.)

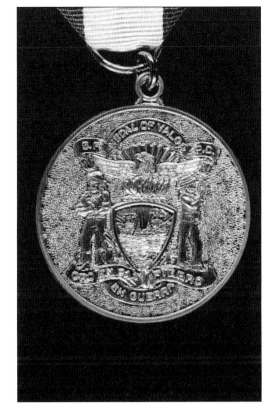

Patrol Special SFPD Officer John Candido received the Law Enforcement Purple Heart for his line-of-duty injury. He started his career working for Frank Alioto at the famous Alioto's No. 8 at Fisherman's Wharf. Then he became a dance-hall cop, worked the Italian Halls in Hunters Point and the Potrero. He even protected Benito Mussolini's pianist brother Romano (who was in the city for a concert) and, later, Cardinal Piero Lachi. Later he had the beat of Laguna to Powell and California Street to Broadway. Since 2000, the SFPD has had its own version of the Purple Heart, which it issues to family members of police officers who have died in the line of duty (Courtesy of the Candido family.)

Officer John Candido was placed in the American Police Hall of Fame, which was founded in 1960. This medal was given to Candido when he was inducted in 1962. The image on the reverse, seen below, depicts Michael the Archangel—leader of the army of God during the Lucifer uprising and the patron saint of police officers. (Courtesy of the Candido family.)

San Francisco 49ers alum Lloyd Winston stands in front of the impressive trophy case at 49ers headquarters in Santa Clara. Winston played for the 49ers during the 1962 and 1963 seasons, under Coach Howard W. "Red" Hickey, and after his football career served in the SFPD for more than 32 years from 1966 to 1998 as a police officer, star 114. He served 15 years at Northern Station, was the traffic cop at Post and Powell—which Herb Caen wrote about due to his antics—and spent nine years in community relations. He grew up in Merced, California, and excelled at fullback at USC. He wore the No. 32 jersey and was a running back for the team before O.J. Simpson wore the same number in 1978–1979. Winston also scored a touchdown for the 49ers during a game in 1963. (Courtesy of the author.)

This January 1963 image shows police bagpipers serenading Pan Am stewardess Imogene Brigden at SFO Airport. The new SFPD Bagpipe Band shows off its outfits, which were flown directly from Scotland via Pan Am's polar route. The officers, from left to right, are Vernon McDowell, Walter Garry, John Jordan, and Lew Werle. (Courtesy of San Francisco History Center, San Francisco Public Library.)

This 1964 image was taken from the back seat of a police car. Seen through the metal screen are policemen Rex Oberg (left) and Sgt. Frank Sturken. Then, as today, committing a crime in San Francisco meant this lovely view of the city would be yours once you were caught. (Courtesy of San Francisco History Center, San Francisco Public Library.)

This *c.* 1964 billboard image was a strong recruiting message. (Courtesy of San Francisco History Center, San Francisco Public Library.)

Three dozen youngsters, ages 3 to 13, walked four miles with Sgt. Joe Galik from the Richmond District through Golden Gate Park to the Sunset District and the home of their pal, Officer Ed P. Lawson in July 1965. Lawson was in a coma for three weeks after he fell off his horse in Golden Gate Park chasing a bicycle thief. He had visited their school every morning for 14 years. (Courtesy of San Francisco History Center, San Francisco Public Library.)

Several members and future members of the SFPD served in the Vietnam War. U.S. Army Specialist No. 4 Anthony Ribera, pictured here, was a future chief of police. As an army military policeman he received his training at Fort Lewis, Washington, and Fort Gordon, Georgia. While in Vietnam from 1967 to 1968 he was assigned to a convoy unit. (Courtesy of SFPD.)

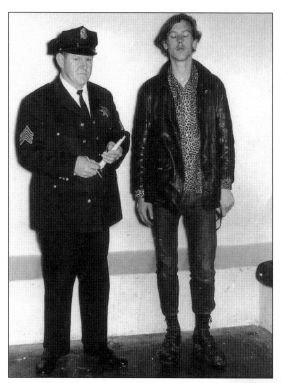

Sgt. Hugh R. O'Connor, star 1382, served in the SFPD from 1941 to 1976. He was well known locally as "Bucky" O'Connor, a former star athlete at St. Mary's College in Moraga when they played "big time" football in the mid-1930s. Like so many San Francisco police officers of that era, he was the son of Irish immigrants. His father, John, was also a member of the SFPD. Hugh attended Lowell High, where he was an all-city guard on the football team. Here, a young man is shown in the "booking" photo with Sgt. O'Connor on April 23, 1967. The photo was taken as part of a mass booking process at Park Station while Sergeant O'Connor acted as watch commander following a peace demonstration in the Haight-Ashbury district. (Courtesy of Dennis John O'Connor.)

Anton Szandor LaVey (1930–1997) was the flamboyant "High Priest of the Church of Satan" and the author of the Satanic Bible. According to that book's introduction, LaVey worked for a while as a photographer for the San Francisco Police Department and, during the Korean War, enrolled in San Francisco City College as a criminology major to avoid the draft. While some believe the legend claiming that LaVey was exposed to the savagery of human nature during his stint as a San Francisco police photographer in the early 1950s, other sources state that the San Francisco Police Department's employment records include no "Howard Levey" or "Anton LaVey." In addition, Frank Moser, who was a SFPD photographer in the early 1950s, said that LaVey never worked for the department. (Courtesy of the author.)

Police officer Richard Radetich was the first graduate of the PAL athletic training program to become a cadet and the first to become an officer, in 1966. This image shows Richard being sworn in by Chief Tom Cahill (right) with star 703. The other individual is believed to be an instructor at the police academy. Prior to this, Richard had briefly attended City College of San Francisco and was an assistant gardener for the City. (Courtesy of the Radetich family.)

Richard was a Boy Scout of Troop 57 in San Francisco. While there, he learned the Scout Oath: "On my honor I will do my best to do my duty to God and my country and to obey the Scout Law; to help other people at all times; to keep myself physically strong, mentally awake, and morally straight." In addition, he followed the Scout Law and was "trustworthy, loyal, helpful, obedient, cheerful and thrifty." Richard attended Balboa High School in San Francisco and graduated in 1961. Some of his Buccaneer teammates had dreams of going to the NFL, but Richard's dream was to be a SFPD officer. From an early age, he never wanted to be anything in life but a policeman. He studied criminology at City College of San Francisco, with the goal of wearing the uniform and seven-pointed star of the SFPD. He was assisted in this endeavor by his mentor and cousin, Ron Radetich of the San Mateo County Sheriffs Department. (Both courtesy of the Radetich family.)

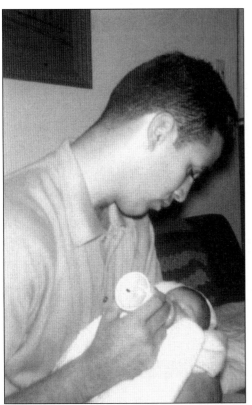

Officer Richard Radetich feeds his eight-month-old daughter Janine, whom he had with wife Nancy. Life was great for the young officer, who had spent four years on the force by 1969. However, Richard never made it to his only child's future wedding, to see that his daughter eventually married a police officer in San Luis Obispo. (Courtesy of the Radetich family.)

Police officer Richard Radetich, just 25 years old, was shot in the head and killed on Friday morning, June 19, 1970, at approximately 5:45 a.m. He was double-parked, alone on the 600 block of Waller Street in the Haight Ashbury, between Scott and Pierce, writing a citation for a vehicle with an expired 1970 tag. Three shots were fired from a .38, and one went through Radetich's left temple. He was found with his microphone in hand and his service revolver in its holster. Richard died at San Francisco General at 8:02 p.m., 15 hours after the shooting. Before he passed away, he endured 6 hours of brain surgery, which required 10 pints of blood. (Courtesy of the Radetich family; photo by Joe Rosenthal.)

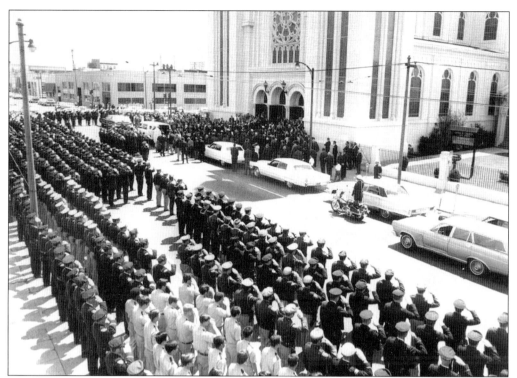

As of 2004, the Radetich murder case is still an open SFPD homicide case; the subject initially arrested had murder charges dropped in January 1971 for this crime. No one else was ever fully charged and the murder case has remained unsolved. Richard Radetich's wife, Nancy, died of cancer in 1974. The SFPD needs the public's assistance to solve the cold-blooded murder of Officer Richard Radetich. If you have any information on this unsolved crime, please call the SFPD Homicide Detail at 415-553-1145 or leave an anonymous tip at 415-431-2127. Also contact the FBI San Francisco office at 415-553-7400 or email sanfrancisco.fbi.gov. (Courtesy of the Radetich family; photo by Joe Rosenthal.)

California governor Ronald Reagan, the future president of the United States of America (1981–1989), wrote this beautiful letter to the Radetich family following Richard's death:

Words cannot truly express my feelings of sorrow for you and your daughter-in-law, but I want you all to know how much I wish there were some way in which I could share your pain. The tragedy that took the life of your son is such a reminder of our imperfections and the frailty of human nature. It isn't given to us to understand why or how such things fit into the divine scheme of things. We can only have faith that we'll be helped, and strength will be given to us in our hours of greatest need. On behalf of millions of citizens of California who entrust their safety to law enforcement officers, I want to express our heartfelt sympathy. You and your family may always cherish the thought of his dedicated public service and the supreme sacrifice he brought for all of us.

The Memorial Wall located in the public lobby at the Hall of Justice at 850 Bryant Street is a tribute to SFPD officers who have died in the line of duty. Show here in 1970 is Harold L. Hamilton's name being carved by the master engraver. The years 1920, 1937, and 1970 were the worst for the SFPD, as four individual officers died in each of those years. Earlier, on February 16, 1970, Officer Brian McDonnell was killed when a bomb exploded at Park Police Station. On August 29, 1971, Sergeant John Young was killed in a barrage of gunfire when two men walk into the Ingleside Police Station and began shooting at officers sitting behind the glass partition. (Courtesy of San Francisco History Center, San Francisco Public Library.)

This 1968 image shows Sgt. Peter Gardner, star 1459, on his last day on the job after having served from 1947 to 1968 at Central, Potrero, and Mission Stations along with traffic. Sergeant Gardner grew up in the Mission District and attended Mission High School. He taught criminology at City College of San Francisco and was the former president of the Police Officers Association, as well as one of the founding members of the Police Credit Union on Irving Street. (Courtesy of San Francisco History Center, San Francisco Public Library.)

Police Chief Alfred J. Nelder (1970–1971) stated that "From the beginning of this decade I promised the citizens of San Francisco that the Police Department will implement three primary goals: (1) place more men and equipment on the street, (2) increase the emphasis on youth programs and (3) improve community relations." He had a sense of history and donated the chief's uniform he designed to the SFPD Police Museum, which, as of this printing is in a non-operational status. Chief Nelder's daughter Amy is currently a crime sketch artist for the SFPD. (Courtesy of San Francisco History Center, San Francisco Public Library.)

This document comes from the FBI file on the Zodiac Killer. Perhaps columnist Warren Hinckle said it best when he wrote, "The Zodiac was a loner who killed and taunted the police in the manner of the Joker in Batman." In the late 1960s a serial killer, who referred to himself as "Zodiac," claimed to have killed 37 people in the San Francisco Bay area. Law enforcement attributes six murders and two attempted murders to Zodiac. Most of the crimes were committed against couples in "lovers' lanes." Zodiac sent letters that included coded messages to local police departments and newspapers. One letter contained squares of blood-stained cloth, cut from the shirt of a victim who was a San Francisco taxi cab driver. Zodiac has never been officially identified. Dave Toschi was the famed lead investigator on the Zodiac case and was with the SFPD for 37 years. (Courtesy of Federal Bureau of Investigation.)

SFPD officers practice the martial art of jui jitsu c. 1970. (Courtesy of San Francisco History Center, San Francisco Public Library.)

"Knock, knock." "Who's there?" "SFPD. Please open up." This dog is man's best friend, crime's worst enemy, protector of the helpless, and defender of the weak. (Courtesy of San Francisco History Center, San Francisco Public Library.)

Two Honda bikes traverse Ocean Beach at the edge of the Pacific Ocean, c. 1970. (Courtesy of SFPD.)

Police Chief Donald M. Scott (third from left) stated, "The SFPD has accepted the challenge of crime in a free society. The men and women of our department, under the capable direction and control of their unit commanders, have faced the challenge with unprecedented vigor and imagination." Under Scott's watch, on July 31, 1972 at 0800 hours, Project CABLE, a dynamic computer system, began. According to an FBI Law Enforcement Bulletin, "CABLE in action clearly demonstrates the results that can be gained toward the improvement of law enforcement through modern technology." In May 1970 it was no longer necessary for SFPD officers to buy their own bullets. They were allotted 18 to cover a one-year period. Any used in the line of duty were replaced for free. The salary for a San Francisco cop in August 1971 was $1,106 per month. They were required to carry a gun off duty as well as on the job, meaning that in essence they were required to be a police officer 24 hours per day. (Courtesy of San Francisco History Center, San Francisco Public Library.)

Police officers ride in Golden Gate Park in the early 1970s in front of the Japanese Tea Garden. The Mounted Unit in the 1970s was conferred a unit citation by President Richard M. Nixon for service rendered on his trip to the city. The unit was also involved during the 1901 President William McKinley visit. Many horses retired to Sonoma, Woodside, or the Sierra Nevada. Horses have endured marbles, beer cans, bottles, and pit bulls, and were even taken into the infamous "Pink Palace" Housing Project at Turk and Scott Streets. (Courtesy of SFPD.)

Two officers run to the helicopter on the roof of the Hall of Justice. In the early 1970s San Francisco had 11 officers assigned to the helicopter program at its peak. School kids named two of the machines in a contest: *Bluebird* and *Phoenix*. The program was disbanded in 1978 and the copters trucked to the L.A. Sheriff's Department only to be reinstituted in the late 1990s, then disbanded again. (Courtesy of San Francisco History Center, San Francisco Public Library.)

This aerial view of the city was taken c. 1970. San Francisco residents complained of the "eye in the sky," and budget restrictions hampered the helicopter program when it was active. (Courtesy of San Francisco History Center, San Francisco Public Library.)

On February 11, 1971, Officer Charles Logasa drowned after his UH-1 Huey helicopter crashed into Lake Merced in 15 feet of water. Patrolman Stan Odmann, the pilot, unhooked Logasa's seatbelt and attempted to rescue the 250-pound officer, to no avail. He was finally pulled out some 40 minutes later. This image shows the helicopter being plucked from the lake. (Courtesy of San Francisco History Center, San Francisco Public Library.)

In January 2000, two more SFPD helicopter officers, Kirk Bradley Brookbush and James Francis Dougherty, died while bringing a copter back from repair. Both men served honorably in the U.S. Armed Forces—Brookbush in the U.S. Army, Vietnam, 75th Ranger Regiment (Airborne) and Dougherty in the U.S. Air Force. Dougherty had also worked as a mechanic for United Airlines. After the 2000 crash, the SFPD helicopter unit was put into inactive status, as it had been from the late 1970s until the 1990s. (Courtesy of SFPD.)

San Francisco Police Department
"Gold in Peace, Iron in War"

In Memoriam

Kirk Bradley Brookbush
September 29, 1950 – January 11, 2000

James Francis Dougherty
May 3, 1943 – January 11, 2000

"Forever Patrolling Our Skies"

Officer W. Beverly, star 1460, poses with his canine (K-9), a Doberman Pinscher named Erich, star 9. On January 24, 1972, Officer Beverly was assassinated by a rifle shot from a window at Twenty-second and Valencia Street. His partner, Jim Bailey, though injured, fired eight shots and the shooter fled. Junious Poole was later convicted of first-degree murder. (Courtesy of SFPD.)

SFPD strongmen posed at the old Sports Palace on Valencia Street in 1973 for Karl Norberg's 80th birthday. Norberg benchpressed 400 pounds in front of, from left to right, Al Feuerbach (Olympian), Nick Ayala, Ray Leso, Don Buck (SFPD), Bill Stathes (SFPD), Dick Notmeyer, Ray Musante (SFPD motorcycle), Ed Lolax, Keith Cain, Karl Norberg, Barry Notmeyer, and Jim Schmitz (three-time Olympic weightlifting coach). (Courtesy of Jim Schmitz.)

This image was taken outside Taraval Station during a four-day police strike in August 1975. Police went on strike because of frustration and what they felt was unfair treatment by politically oriented officials in an election year. In the first eight hours of the strike there was not a single arrest made in San Francisco! Supervisor Diane Feinstein was perturbed with the armed picketers outside the Hall of Justice and wanted them disarmed. Mayor Joe Alioto initially played hardball and said "If there is a strike, I have said before, I am going to recommend immediate suspension without pay of any policeman who strikes and a hearing after which, if the facts are found correctly, they will be fired." The SFPD wanted a 13 percent increase in pay, the mayor gave them 9 percent, and the strike was over in four days. (Courtesy of Dennis John O'Connor.)

Police Chief Charles Gain (1975–1980) was appointed by Mayor George R. Moscone. Gain usually wore a suit instead of a police uniform. During his tenure, some members of the department did not agree with his management style. Gain ordered all the black-and-white patrol cars be painted "baby blue and white," and according to street cops, "the criminals laughed at them." He removed the seven-pointed star on the car doors, replacing it with "police services," and allegedly took the American flag out of his chief's office so as "not to intimidate people." He was criticized for having his photo taken with Jim Jones, of the People's Temple, who later committed mass suicide with 900 followers in the jungles of Guyana. During his career Gain also served as police chief of Oakland, California. It was during this time, in 1976, that then-student Osama bin Laden lived at the Gramercy Towers at 1177 California Street. (Courtesy of San Francisco History Center, San Francisco Public Library.)

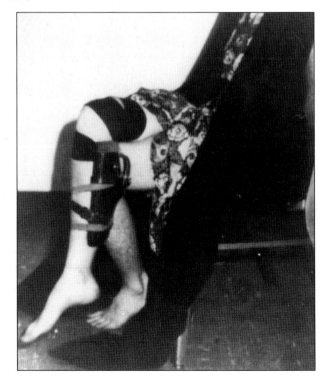

Charles Manson initially recruited Lynette Squeeky Fromme into his "Family" in the Haight-Ashbury district. This photo shows where she hid her gun when she pointed it at President Ford September 1975 in Sacramento. Just 17 days later another assassination attempt took place in San Francisco. The red-haired Fromme wore a bright red dress to symbolize blood. (Courtesy of Gerald R. Ford Library, Ann Arbor, Michigan, and U.S. Secret Service)

Abducted newspaper heiress and later fugitive bank robber Patty Hearst, who had been kidnapped and held for 19 months by the Symbionese Liberation Army (SLA), was captured at 625 Morse Street in San Francisco's outer Mission District. She was wanted in the April 1974 robbery of $10,000 from the Hibernia Bank in the Sunset District. Hearst lived at this address for two weeks with Wendy Yoshimura. Retired SFPD cop Raymond Ray, who had also worked with the Bureau of Criminal Identification, was the listing broker at Cutino Realty and had accepted a rental agreement for that address dated "9-9-1975" signed by "Charles Adams." Upon discovering the identity of the tenants, Ray said, "I spent 20 years in the SFPD. I guess I've lost my cop's eye, but then, I guess they have been doing pretty well staying out of sight for the last year or so." Later, SFPD Officer Bernard Shaw, working off-duty for the Hearst family, fell in love with Patricia Hearst, and they married. Shaw is now director of Hearst Corporation Security. (Courtesy of the author.)

President Gerald R. Ford had just finished a luncheon address to the Commonwealth Club on Monday, September 22, 1975, and exited the north side of the Saint Francis Hotel on the 400 block of Post Street at Powell when a shot rang out at 3:30 p.m. from the north side of Post Street. The SFPD officer to the left of President Ford is Gary Lemos (with moustache) and behind him is Sgt. Dave Winn. The gun was purchased for $125 in Danville, California, by the unsuccessful assassin Sara Jane Moore, who pulled the weapon out of her purse. Moore, an FBI informant and professional accountant, was also a middle-class mom with four kids and was married to a medical doctor. (Courtesy of Gerald R. Ford Library, Ann Arbor, Michigan, and U.S. Secret Service.)

Policeman Timothy Hettrich grabbed the .38 Smith and Wesson away from 45-year-old Sara Jane Moore after San Franciscan Oliver Sipple intervened, making it impossible for her to fire another shot. Hettrich was joined by Secret Service agent Dotson Reeves, Officers Frank Reed and Phil Bill, Inspector Frank Ree, and Sgt. Gary Lemos. The slug hit the façade of the Saint Francis Hotel; a piece that broke off then hit cabbie John Ludwig who received a superficial wound. (Courtesy of Gerald R. Ford Library, Ann Arbor, Michigan, and U.S. Secret Service.)

This Secret Service sequence photo shows the action taken after the assassination attempt on President Ford. Author John Garvey, then a 13-year-old student at nearby Notre Dame des Victories, was an eyewitness to this assassination attempt while standing on the curb on Union Square. (Courtesy of Gerald R. Ford Library, Ann Arbor, Michigan, and U.S. Secret Service.)

This San Francisco Airport tarmac photo shows the congratulatory praise President Ford gave the SFPD after the assassination attempt. White House aide James H. Falk designated Northern California as "kook capital of the world" after two apparent efforts to assassinate President Ford in just 17 days. (Courtesy of Gerald R. Ford Library, Ann Arbor, Michigan, and U.S. Secret Service.)

This Secret Service target, c. 1975, from the Old Mint shooting range at Fifth and Mission shows that the SFPD and U.S. Secret Service were ready for the assassination attempt. Sara Jane Moore was sentenced to life in federal prison. The June 1976 issue of *Playboy* magazine featured an article on Moore and a photo of her reading the front page of the September 23, 1975 *San Francisco Chronicle* about her history-making action. Lawrence H. Lawler, a former Oakland police officer and special agent in charge of the San Francisco FBI office from August 1975 to March 1979, was later responsible for the investigation of the assassination attempt on Gerald Ford, the kidnapping of Patty Hearst, and the Jonestown massacre in Guyana. (Courtesy of the author.)

September 25, 1975

Dear Mr. Sipple:

I want you to know how much I appreciated your
selfless actions last Monday. The events were
a shock to us all, but you acted quickly and
without fear for your own safety. By doing so
you helped to avert danger to me and to others
in the crowd. You have my heartfelt appreciation.

Sincerely,

Mr. Oliver W. Sipple
334 Leavenworth Street
San Francisco, California

GRF:AVH;JC;ec

cc: Jack Hushen

On September 25, 1975 this White House thank you letter was sent to U.S. Marine PFC Oliver Sipple for his help during the assassination attempt on President Ford. Immediately after he saved the president's life Sipple said to the media, "Leave out that Marine stuff. I'm no hero or nothing. I never got any medals. I was in for three-and-a-half-years and I'm retired on a full pension. Well, I have some shrapnel." Sipple later experienced discrimination from the media, who made an issue over his sexual orientation. (Courtesy of Gerald R. Ford Library, Ann Arbor, Michigan.)

PFC Oliver "Billy" W. Sipple, USMC, is buried at Golden Gate National Cemetery, 1300 Sneath Lane, San Bruno, CA, Section T, Row 0, Grave 2268. He is buried in a sacred field with other American patriots. His heroic action in helping to prevent the assassination of President Gerald R. Ford on Post Street greatly assisted the SFPD and the nation. SFPD Investigator Jack Webb determined the single bullet fired came within inches of President Ford's head. Sipple's grave joins 112,900 other soldiers and their families in the 28-acre marble orchard in San Bruno. (Courtesy of the author.)

This September 1977 *San Francisco Chronicle* front page describes the Golden Dragon Restaurant Massacre at Grant and Jackson. The massacre left 5 dead and 11 wounded and was carried out by the most violent Asian gang in U.S. history. Future SFPD chiefs Fred Lau and Heather Fong helped to identify and successfully prosecute the murderers. Years later, in July 1993, a disgruntled client named Gian Luigi Ferri, armed with two TEC-9 assault weapons, stormed the downtown law firm of Pettit & Martin and other offices at 101 California Street, killing 8 people and wounding 6. These weapons had been purchased from a pawnshop and a gun show in Nevada. Ferri killed himself after that murder spree. (Courtesy of the Barisone family.)

This 1978 image shows Britain's Prince Charles at the Fairmont Hotel on Nob Hill shaking the hand of, from left to right, Sgt. Dave Winn and Officers Ken Hartman, Bob Del Torre, Bill Taylor, and Joe De Renzi. Prince Charles was three hours late leaving town because he would not leave until he personally shook the hand of every officer who provided his security protection during his visit. (Courtesy of SFPD.)

Lt. Tony Ribera, star 418, briefs officers at the old Mission Station on Valencia Street, c. 1980. Ribera is a native of San Francisco who attended Sacred Heart High School and George Washington High School. (Courtesy of SFPD.)

This 1980 group photo of the SFPD Honda Unit, taken in front of the Conservatory of Flowers, shows, from left to right, patrolmen Bob Derby, Dave O'Donnell, Jim O'Shea, Wayne Smith, Dick Sheehan, Jerry Donovan, John Hennessy, Mike Chase, George Cima, Bob Del Torre, Mike Lawson, and Sgt. Julian Landman, making an even dozen. (Courtesy of SFPD.)

Dan White was a policeman, a fireman, and a city supervisor. On November 27, 1978 he murdered Mayor George Moscone and Supervisor Harvey Milk. Large groups of gay men and others rioted on the night of May 21, 1979, after a jury returned a verdict of voluntary homicide, sentencing White to serve just five years. Later that night the SPFD launched its infamous raid of the Elephant Walk establishment in the Castro District. After his release, White returned to Ireland, then came back to the United States, and even enjoyed the boxing competition at the 1984 L.A. Olympics. Life was never the same, however, and he committed suicide. One of his favorite songs, "The Town I Loved So Well," was playing in the car at the time of his death. (Courtesy of San Francisco History Center, San Francisco Public Library.)

The famed SFPD Park Unit was formed in May 1981 at the urging of Mayor Diane Feinstein and was disbanded in May 1991. From left to right, at Angler's Lodge in Golden Gate Park, are (standing) Officers Dan May, Ron Roth, Bob Del Torre, and Sgt. Jim "Beetle" Bailey (kneeling). The firepower shown here is only part of the story as this elite group has on record 9,980 arrests in a 10-year period of patrolling all city parks, playgrounds, and recreational centers. They recovered 85 guns and hundreds of knives and homemade weapons. This was a big change in Golden Gate Park since police were put on motorbikes in 1902 to enforce a 15-mph limit on a one-cylinder Rambler. (Courtesy of SFPD.)

Mother Teresa (1910–1997) is shown here with the SFPD on May 28, 1987 outside Saint Dominic's Church while attending an event where nuns were making their first vows. Born in what is now Skopje, Macedonia, this Roman Catholic nun created positive change on behalf of the world's poor, founding the Sisters of Charity whose mission is the relief of human suffering. She was awarded the Nobel Peace Prize in 1979 for her work and was beatified in October 2003. (Courtesy of the Candido family.)

Sgt. John Macaulay Park, at Larkin and O'Farrell Streets, was named for a highly decorated officer who was shot in the head and killed by an armed robber on July 17, 1982. The fenced-in park was renovated in 2003 and now is an oasis for the 3,000 children of the Tenderloin, an area known for cheap rents, the sex trade, homelessness, and drugs. It has always been a rough area. Officers who were assigned here were paid more and could afford the tenderloin cut of beef. The term "tenderloin" originated in New York City in a depraved area called "Satan's Circus," and was coined by Capt. Alexander Williams of the NYPD in 1876. This park is across the street from a gentlemen's club and near several bars, liquor stores, and massage establishments. The club was raided by SFPD vice officers in May 2004 and its general manager was charged with "keeping a house of ill repute." (Courtesy of the author.)

San Francisco Police Centurions included, from left to right, Sgt. Mike Lawson (No.23), Sgt. Bob Del Torre (No. 86), and Greg Suhr (No. 76). Del Torre caught seven passes in this February 20, 1982 game against the San Jose Police Choirboys at PAL Stadium in San Jose. Lawson was CCSF defensive player of the year in 1972. Suhr played at Saint Ignatius in the Sunset District. He is now deputy chief and runs the patrol force. In ancient Rome, Centurions were commanding officers of a Roman century, being a military unit of 100 men. (Courtesy of SFPD.)

From left to right are Sgt. Peter Gardner (retired), star 1459; his son Dan, star 1459 (Northern Station); his son Matt, star 671 (Park Station); and Police Chief Cornelius P. Murphy. This c.1980 photo was taken during Matt's SFPD Academy graduation at Silver Avenue. Police Chief Cornelius P. Murphy (1980–1986) stated, "My top priority is to decrease the incidents of on-street crime by increasing the visibility of our patrol force. I will assign more officers to the district stations for foot patrol duty as soon as sufficient numbers of recruits graduate from the Police Academy. I also intend to increase the strength of our Park and Beach unit and the solo motorcycle unit." In May 1983 Murphy started the Fingerprints on File program to be used as a tool for locating and identifying missing children. At age 18 the children's fingerprints are destroyed along with their optional photograph. (Courtesy of SFPD.)

Police Chief Frank Jordan (1986–1990) beat out Mayor Art Agnos for the mayor's job. Born and raised in San Francisco, Jordan went to Sacred Heart High School and holds a degree in political science and government from the University of San Francisco. He also has a teaching credential and has received several Police Officer of the Year awards. (Courtesy of SFPD.)

Pictured here are Clint Eastwood and Mayor Art Agnos, a victim of the Zebra murders. The Zebra killers randomly shot Caucasians in the San Francisco Bay area during a 1973–1974 spree that left 14 people dead. They were dubbed the Zebra killings because of the radio channel used by the police investigating the case (channel Z). This spree, committed by black members of an offshoot of the Muslim religion, was an attempt by the murderers to win "Death Angel" status. This dubious honor was given to any "true believer" who murdered a certain number of whites, with more credit awarded for slaying a child or woman than a man supposedly because it took more fortitude to do so. Operation Zebra caught four African Americans who were arrested, convicted, and given life sentences in Judge Karesh's courtroom. Detectives Gus Coreris and John Fotinos, both 13-year veterans of the Homicide Unit, led the investigation that eventually cracked the case. Agnos, a member of the California Commission on Aging, was attending a community meeting in a black neighborhood to discuss building a government-funded health clinic in the area. As the meeting let out, Agnos stopped to talk with two women. One of the killers came up behind him and shot him twice in the back. Bystanders called an ambulance and Agnos barely survived. Eastwood played SFPD Inspector Harry Callaghan in *Magnum Force* (1970), *Dirty Harry* (1971), *Sudden Impact* (1983), and *Dead Pool* (1988). Over 30 SFPD officers played themselves in the film *Dead Pool*. Eastwood's SFPD star 2211 was the same throughout all four films and is worn today by solo motorcycle officer Lt. Robert Armani. (Courtesy of San Francisco History Center, San Francisco Public Library.)

SFPD Officer Bob Geary, star 2046, is pictured with his puppet partner Officer Brendan O'Smarty, star ½, just 34 inches tall and weighing 10 pounds. Geary's idea for his puppet partner was a direct result of a community police class he took in 1990 on imaginative ways to reach the public. Geary picked up this puppet via mail order and started to bring him on his beat. His irate supervisors instructed him to get rid of the puppet. In 1993, some 68,000 San Franciscans voted on Measure BB to allow Officer Geary to carry Officer O'Smarty on duty. Both retired in style on July 12, 2000 as they climbed into a horse-drawn carriage and lead a procession to Pier 39 with the famous Green Street Mortuary Band. After a final salute from colleagues, they got on a boat and sailed under the Golden Gate Bridge. (Courtesy of Terence Laubach.)

Isiah "Ike" Nelson III, star 869, died on his motorcycle on the freeway that was being repaired following the 1989 Loma Prieta earthquake. The Isiah Nelson Spirit Award was instituted in 1990 by the San Francisco Giants front office to memorialize the late SFPD commander, who was in charge of the Candlestick Park police detail in 1989. The recipient of this annual award is selected by San Francisco Giants management as the employee who exhibits the true characteristics of Commander Nelson, an outstanding professional who performed his duties with spirit and dedication. (Courtesy of SFPD.)

Officer Brian Danker, star 582, and his partner, Officer Bruce Fairbairn, star 679, are shown outside Potrero Station in 1991. Danker is the cousin of the famous Irish Uprising fugitive O'Connel, whose sons came to America. One became a Secret Service agent and the other a New York City fireman. While in the U.S. Army in Vietnam, Danker was awarded the Bronze Star. He lent his .44 to Clint Eastwood for the 1988 film *Dead Pool* and the weapon was ceremoniously presented to Eastwood after the film. Danker and Fairbairn graduated from the police academy together in 1984. (Courtesy of SFPD.)

Police Chief Willis Casey (1990–1992) was born and raised in San Francisco. Casey spent two years in the U.S. Army before joining the SFPD, working his way up the ladder to make chief. After a brief retirement he served as chief of the Pittsburgh, California Police Department and in the Contra Costa County sheriff's office, then as Pittsburgh's city manager. He was succeeded by Police Chief Richard Hongisto, who held the position for only 42 days. Chief Tom Walsh, Chief William J. Quinn's immediate predecessor, has Hongisto beat—Walsh was cheif for only one day. (Courtesy of San Francisco History Center, San Franscisco Public Library.)

When the May 7, 1992 edition of the *Bay Times* hit newsstands, Hongisto was outraged to see his head on the body of Peggy Sue, an out-front activist in the city during the late 1980s and 1990s. Inside the newspaper, an article by newsman Tim Kingston criticized Hongisto's handling of public reaction on the streets of San Francisco after the not guilty verdicts against police officers in the Rodney King beating trial in Los Angeles. Two thousand people were arrested in San Francisco, where Mayor Frank Jordan declared a state of emergency and a

curfew after looters struck downtown stores in the days after the King verdict. Hongisto, Jordan, and others decided to ban all public demonstrations outright. When marchers gathered at Twenty-fourth and Mission Streets on May 1, Hongisto ordered them dispersed. Hundreds were arrested in the confrontation. Hongisto, a native San Franciscan, previously was sheriff of San Francisco and police chief of Cleveland. (Courtesy of San Francisco History Center, San Francisco Public Library.)

Police Chief Anthony "Tony" Ribera (1992–1996) instituted a police academy for private citizens and was behind the confiscating of automobiles used by clients to pick up prostitutes on the streets of San Francisco. In 1993 he ordered all city police officers to receive SWAT-like training as a result of the 101 California Street office massacre, in which eight people were killed. In 1995 Ribera oversaw a program organized by Capt. Tim Hettrich of Potrero Station that swapped guns for computers at Third and Newcomb Streets. The idea was to get young people's fingers off the trigger and onto the computer keyboard. Ribera walked on foot everyday to Saint Patrick's Church to attend Mass and directed traffic during firefighting operations. Dr. Ribera is now the director of the International Institute of Criminal Justice Leadership at the University of San Francisco. He has a Ph.D. in public administration from Golden Gate University. (Courtesy of SFPD.)

San Francisco Police Department
"Gold in Peace, Iron in War"

In Memoriam

Officer James Louis Guelff

February 27, 1956 - November 14, 1994

Police Officer James Louis Guelff, star 1461, is memorialized on a commemorative sidewalk plaque at Pine and Franklin Streets. The 10-year veteran was killed in a 25-minute shootout with gunman Victor Boutwell, who fired more than 200 rounds of ammunition from five weapons and injured three other people before he was taken out by a police SWAT team. The 38-year-old Guelff (1956–1994), armed only with a department-issued six-shot revolver was shot in the head as he attempted to reload his weapon during the gun fight. Initially assigned to the old Northern Station on Ellis Street for field training after being appointed to the SFPD on his birthday in 1984, Guelff was later transferred to Ingleside. In August 1985 he returned to Northern Station at its new location on Turk Street. Guelff earned a bronze medal of valor and 40 Captain Complimentaries. He is buried at Mount Tamalpais Cemetery in San Rafael. (Courtesy of SFPD.)

Shown here on Saint Patrick's Day in 1995 on McAllister Street are (left) Mike Philpott, now star 65, and Deputy Chief of Police Diarmuid Philpott, star 65 here. Their father faught with Michael Collins for a free Ireland. Mike has his dad's star number, which was also his grandfather's number. Diarmuid's son Brian, star 925, also serves on the force. (Courtesy of SFPD.)

114

This *c.* 1995 image from Potrero Station shows (left) Bart Johnson, star 1024, and Kevin Whitfield, star 493. Johnson has two other brothers in the department who served with Mayor Willie Brown Jr.'s detail—Anthony, star 2233, and Cornelius, star 2176. (Courtesy of SFPD.)

The Potrero Station personnel in this *c.* 1995 image are, from left to right, Officers Kitt Crenshew, William Carlin, Steve Jones, Gregory Lynch, Ike Henry (painting the sergeant's office that day), Wayne Smith, Dennis Meixner, and Bill Davenport—the beloved captain of Southern Station, who passed away in 2004 of cancer. (Courtesy of SFPD.)

Police Chief Fred Lau (1996–2002) appears with Officer Brian Danker, star 582, who was awarded the silver Medal of Valor for his actions at the Guelff shooting. Chief Lau is remembered as a man who visits his sick and wounded officers, on his own time, even when retired. As of this writing, Lau is the Transportation Security Administration's federal security director at Metropolitan Oakland International Airport. (Courtesy of SFPD.)

Sgt. Ken Cottura, star 1877, and author John Garvey are pictured at a graduation ceremony of the San Francisco Citizen's Police Academy No. 4 in Diamond Heights, May 1996, during Chief Lau's term when the notorious "Spiderman" (who was believed responsible for 63 burglaries across the Sunset District) was caught. The civilian program covers procedures from patrol and investigations, vehicle operations, arrest and control techniques, firearm procedures, and communications/911. The academy's goal is to develop community awareness through education and a closer understanding and working relationship between the San Francisco Police Department and the communities it serves. The academy features a ride-along in a police car, the brainchild of Police Chief Tony Ribera. Courtesy of SFPD.)

The SFPD boat *SF Marine 1* is shown here at Yerba Buena Island. The SFPD also has a zodiac craft at the Hyde Street Wharf. (Courtesy of SFPD.)

Capt. George Stasko II (1951–1999), known to his friends as "Jake," died when his car struck a tree as he drove home to Santa Rosa following a bank robbery in downtown San Francisco. He was 47. Buried at Calvary Cemetery in Petaluma, Stasko won two silver medals and eight bronze medals for valor and over 350 Captain Commendations. Stasko headed up the special operations division, which includes the department's SWAT team. Stasko and his twin brother "Sgt. Mike" grew up in Noe Valley. Both brothers attended St. Mary's College and joined the SFPD in 1977. George Stasko tutored and mentored kids with his Operation Dream and started a food and toy drive that now provides a toy for every child in public housing. He also took kids fishing and skiing up in Tahoe. (Courtesy of SFPD.)

San Francisco Police Department

Gold in Peace, Iron in War

Captain George Stephen Stasko II
May 1, 1951 – January 16, 1999

Sgt. Mary Dunnigan, star 99, is seen onsite at "Ground Zero," the ruins of the World Trade Center in New York City with Lt. Joe Zinck (Boston PD), Chaplain Deputy Glen George (Akron, Ohio), and Mike Shea (SFPD, star 1962). Sgt. Dunnigan was part of a SFPD response team dispatched to the incident. She now works in the SFPD Behavioral Science Unit at Treasure Island. (Courtesy of SFPD.)

Cunningham police brothers, from left to right, Dan (star 650), Jim (star 236), and Neil (star 655) are shown with their mother, Dolores, and father, Con. In 1996, Dan nabbed *America's Most Wanted* fugitive Charles Yancey, wanted for a grisly 1992 murder on Manhattan's Lower East Side, with partners Gary Constantine, star 524, and Robert Leung (star 2210). The fugitive, who was profiled on *America's Most Wanted* for five years, was caught at the Hayes Valley South housing project at Page and Webster Streets. All three went to Saint Cecilia Grammar School, graduated from Archbishop Riordan High School in San Francisco, and were in the San Francisco Sheriff's Department at the same time in the 1980s. They were the first three brothers to be in the sheriff's department at the same time. (Courtesy of SFPD.)

This June 2002 image of the softball team, from left to right, includes (front row) Bob Del Torre, Warren Hawes, Glen Ortega, Jim McCoy, Jim Drago, and Dave Herman; (back row) Jack Minkel, Gary Delagnes, Daniel Del Torre (batboy), Matt Hanley, Greg Latus, Jim O'Meara, Ross Laflin, and Ralph Labutan. The SFPD has several sports teams, including an ice hockey team. (Courtesy of SFPD.)

From left to right are Chief Fred Lau, Officer and Mrs. John Candido, and Deputy Chief Earl Sanders, who was holding a dinner party to celebrate his promotion to deputy chief in 2003. Chief Prentice E. Sanders, also known as Earl Sanders, was the first African American to hold the rank of chief of the SFPD. Sanders played a prominent role in the founding of Officers for Justice, an organization formed to end discrimination and bigotry in the San Francisco Police Department. In 1978, then Inspector Sanders testified on behalf of Officers for Justice in a federal court case accusing the city's police department with failing to hire minorities and women and also endangering the lives of minorities on the force. (Courtesy of SFPD.)

Pictured at the 2003 Korean War Remembrance Day in San Francisco are Gen. Alfred Gray, the 29th commandant of the Marine Corps (1987–1990); SFPD Chief Alex Fagan Sr. (2003–2004); and author John Garvey. Fagan graduated from UC Berkeley with a degree in criminology in 1972 and joined the force the following year. In 1979 he swam 200 yards to help save a suicidal woman in San Francisco Bay. He is credited with saving 30 men during a Folsom Barracks gay bathhouse fire in 1976. Fagan also worked as an inspector and spent time in the narcotics unit, the homicide detail, and fiscal unit. Prior to being chief he was the captain at Northern Station. (Courtesy of the author.)

Claudia Curran (left), the great-grandniece of SFPD Officer Edward Maloney, who was killed in the line of duty, is pictured here with Chief Heather Fong, the first female chief in SFPD history. San Francisco mayor Gavin Newsom made history by appointing both female fire and police chiefs in 2004. Fong, a San Francisco native who speaks Cantonese fluently, joined the force in 1977 after graduating from the University of San Francisco. At USF she joined the police reserves and received a commission in the Air Force Reserve. She became one of the first three women promoted to captain in 1994 and, in 1996, she became one of the first two women to head a district police station. Later she became commander of the special operations division, which includes the SWAT team, then became the deputy chief and chief. She has participated with the department's famous Lion Dance Team in the world famous Chinese New Year Parade. She is the first Asian woman and only the eighth woman ever to take the helm of a big city police department. (Courtesy of the author.)

Sgt. Bob Del Torre (star 2043), a 32-year veteran of the force, is pictured at Treasure Island with the San Francisco skyline in the background of this 2003 image. He is a member of the American Police Hall of Fame, was California Outstanding Public Safety Officer of the Year, and in 2002 was awarded the prestigious California Peace Officers "Award of Law Enforcement Profession Achievement" by Attorney General Bill Lockyer. He has been awarded an incredible 14 Medals of Valor and has been injured 31 times in the line of duty. During his last five years in the SFPD he made 550 narcotic arrests, 220 robbery arrests, and confiscated 175 weapons. He even found time to win the gold medal in the men's discus throw in the 2002 California State Police Games in Stockton. He was also in the movie *Cool Runnings*, playing a bobsledder, and was a member of the U.S. bobsled team. (Courtesy of SFPD.)

Officer Kelvin Tso, star 602, is shown in 2004 with the SFPD's specialized bicycle patrol at San Francisco's new international airport terminal. The $1 billion showpiece opened in November 2000 and is the largest international terminal in North America. The airport handles over 40 million passengers per year and ranks as the fifth busiest airport in America. (Courtesy of SFPD.)

Officer Phil Welsh (star 1861) of Central Station poses with a beautiful Irish lass and handsome lad at the start of the 2004 Saint Patrick's Day Parade at Second and Market Streets Welsh was this author's baseball coach at Notre Dame des Victories in the early 1970s. (Courtesy of the author.)

Officer Nick Shihadeh (star 1612) of Park Station and sports editor of the *POA Journal* is shown at the 2004 Saint Patrick's Day Parade at Second and Market Streets. Since 2003 all officers in the SFPD have the option of using non-lethal force with "Super Sock" bean bags. These beanbags may be used against suspects who, while dangerous, may be able to be subdued without a gun. After Officer Guelff's murder in 1994, the SFPD exchanged the six-bullet .357 magnum Smith and Wesson for the 17-bullet 9mm Beretta. The latter weapon did not have the stopping ability of the Sig-Sauer .40 caliber, 11-bullet gun carried today. Officer Shihadeh was once shot point blank in the chest and was saved by the bulletproof vest. The bullet was deflected and nicked his chin, and he was able to return fire on his assailant. (Courtesy of the author.)

This 2004 image shows a Koban in Japantown; operational Kobans are also on Grant Avenue and at the Powell Street cable car turnaround. Recently the SFPD has relinquished this community policing tool to private security guards who provide informational services. Today the city is divided up into ten companies: Central, Southern, Bayview, Mission, Northern, Park, Richmond, Ingleside, Taraval, and Tenderloin. Mayor Gavin Newsom, a fifth-generation San Franciscan, is the great-great-grandson of a carpenter, who himself served in the SFPD after he arrived in the city in the 1880s. (Courtesy of the author.)

This unidentified officer films a march up Market Street held in observance of the one-year anniversary of the Iraq war, on March 18, 2004. (Courtesy of the author.)

Officer Christi McCall, star 3004, poses with two youngsters in this March 17, 2004 photo. McCall is a member of the SFPD Reserve, which has about 30 members and an authorized strength of over 900 per the city charter. To join the reserve, which works events like parades, contact the SFPD. For many years the SFPD Reserve was at 2310 Third Street. (Courtesy of the author.)

The four Pengel sisters who concurrently serve in the SFPD are, from left to right, Maura Pengel, star 1332, Mission Station; Lt. Miriam Pengel, star 1553, Richmond Station; Lt. Molly Pengel, star 2187, Taraval; and Deputy Chief Mindy Pengel, star 2076, Airport Bureau. In the center is their proud dad, Officer Henry "Hank" Pengel, star 1553, who retired as an inspector. Lt. Miriam Pengel has her father's star number. This is believed to be a law enforcement world record for the most female siblings; Boston Police Department's Inspector Arthur Pugsley had his record seven police officer sons with him on the force. (Courtesy of SFPD.)

Officer Billy Ray Smith (star 202) of SFPD's Bayview Station, is the head coach of this 2004 SF Striders and Lady Striders Youth Track and Field Club. Smith coaches the youngsters at the Philip and Sala Burton Academic High School (the old Wilson High School) and has been a fixture in youth sports and in the lives of many young people all over the San Francisco Bay area. He is assisted in this rewarding activity by Duane Breaux. The SF Striders' motto is "to promote fitness instead of drugs." Many young people are drawn to Smith's program, whose initials "SF" stand for "Scholastics First!" as well as San Francisco. The name "Striders" stands for Striving Toward Responsible Individual Development Education Respect and Self-esteem. The Striders program affords youth opportunities for positive interactions with law enforcement officers, adults, and their peers while providing a safe environment to travel and compete in athletics across the United States. (Courtesy of the author.)

Jim Speros, star 436 (retired), is the senior police advisor for police media and community relations to the Ministry of the Interior of Iraq. In the ministry system, Interior runs the police service nationwide. Speros mentors his counterparts in the Iraq Police Service so they develop national policy and ownership of their process and can guide its growth and the positive future of their nation. This photo was taken in front of the family fishpond at Saddam Hussein's former palace, now the U.S. Embassy. Speros retired in 2002 after 28 years in policing, the last 22 with the SFPD. He wrote the city's community policing strategic plan in 1994 and coordinated its implementation from 1992 to 1998. He was also SFPD training coordinator with Amsterdam and South Africa and founded the SFPD portion of "Climate of Trust" in 1999, a partnership with Russia that presents symposiums on hate crimes and community policing. When he retired he moved to British Columbia. Speros continues to do volunteer work with the RCMP. He was with the Belmont Police from 1976 to 1979 and the SF State College Police from 1974 to 1976. (Courtesy of SFPD.)

An unidentified SFPD officer renders a salute as the body of Officer Isaac Espinoza is taken from Saint Mary's Cathedral to the waiting hearse for final burial at Holy Cross Catholic Cemetery. Espinoza left a wife, Renata, and a three-year-old child, Isabella. Officer Walter Ware was interviewed on Channel 2 News on May 1, 2004 after he and several officers donated their time and skills to finish the back deck and fence at the Espinoza home that officer Espinoza had left unfinished following his murder on April 10, 2004. (Courtesy of the author.)

Officer Isaac Anthony Espinoza, star 64, (July 16, 1974–April 10, 2004) was assassinated with an AK-47. His Mass card read as follows:

I AM FREE. Don't grieve for me, for now I'm free. I am following the path God has laid for me. I took his hands when I heard him call. I turned my back and left it all. I could not stay another day, to laugh, to love, to work, or play. Tasks left undone must stay that way. I found that peace at the close of day. If my parting has left a void, then fill it with remembered joy. A friendship shared, a laugh, a kiss, it is these things I too will miss. Be not burdened with time of sorrow. I wish to you the sunshine of tomorrow. My life's been full, I savored such good friends, good times, a loved one's touch. Perhaps my time seemed all too brief, don't lengthen it now with undue grief. Lift up your hearts and share with me. God wanted me. HE SET ME FREE.

(Courtesy of SFPD.)

126

LINE OF DUTY DEATHS

The following officers lost their lives while on duty:

1. John Coots, June 12, 1878
2. John Nicholson, February 16, 1884
3. Edgar Osgood, December 13, 1886
4. Alexander Grant, September 11, 1891
5. William Burke, March 23, 1898
6. Eugene Robinson, January 20, 1903
7. Max Fenner, April 18, 1906
8. William H. Heins, 1906
9. James S. Cook, August 26, 1906
10. George O'Connell, November 16, 1906
11. Harry L. Sauer, May 7, 1907
12. Edward T. McCarthey, September 3, 1907
13. William O'Shaughnessy, June 10, 1908
14. Antone Nelting, January 9, 1909
15. Charles F. Castor, November 26, 1911
16. Thomas Finnelly, November 26, 1911
17. John J. Nolan, March 19, 1912
18. Charles H. Bates, July 26, 1912
19. Byron C. Wood, May 4, 1913
20. Edward Maloney, April 19, 1915
21. Peter Hammond, May 12, 1915
22. Frederick Cook, November 24, 1915
23. Thomas Deasy, January 8, 1916
24. Martin Judge, December 12, 1916
25. William F. Sheehan, June 25, 1917
26. John B. Hurd, January 27, 1918
27. John J. Moriarity, May 26, 1919
28. Antone Schoembs, November 19, 1920
29. James W. Horton, September 19, 1920
30. Miles Jackson, December 5, 1920
31. Lester Dorman, December 5, 1920
32. Thomas Hanna, January 15, 1921
33. Thomas Walsh, July 4, 1922

34. Timothy Bailey, August 3, 1922
35. Thomas Kelly, June 4, 1923
36. Joseph Conroy, November 3, 1923
37. Michael J. Brady, October 5, 1924
38. George Campbell, April 9, 1925
39. Benjamin G. Root, April 1, 1926
40. John J. Driscoll, June 28, 1927
41. Frederick Nuttman, December 31, 1927
42. Frederick N. Spooncer, November 24, 1928
43. John Malcom, April 29, 1930
44. Charles Rogerson, November 23, 1930
45. Charles W. King, June 7, 1931
46. Elmer C. Thoney, December 31, 1931
47. William E. Manning, January 1, 1932
48. Mervyn A. Reardon, June 9, 1932
49. Michael J. McDonald, August 26, 1933
50. James H. Mann, February 26, 1934
51. Edward F. Flagler, February 8, 1937
52. Albert W. Argens, February 21, 1937
53. Cornelius Brosnan, November 15, 1937
54. Waldemar L. Jentzsch, December 25, 1937
55. Walter Salisbuty, January 1, 1939
56. Vincent F. Lynch, August 30, 1941
57. Timothy Ryan, February 11, 1943
58. Phillip T. Farshman, March 3, 1946
59. William J. Bowman, January 1, 1948
60. Richard J. Scholz, September 19, 1948
61. Robert L. Walters, September 27, 1952
62. Denis Bradley, October 8, 1953
63. Thomas J. Guzzetti, January 1, 1955
64. Henry J. Eidler, May 28, 1955
65. Gordon J. Oliveria, December 31, 1955

66. Joseph Lacey, December 31, 1956
67. Robert J. Morey, August 8, 1958
68. Barry R. Rosekind, August 16, 1958
69. William C. Long, August 21, 1958
70. James Mancusi, Jr., June 18, 1965
71. Herman L. George, November 13, 1967
72. Peter McElligott, June 19, 1968
73. Rene G. Lacau, April 17,1969
74. Joseph Brodnick, May 1, 1969
75. Eric A. Zelms, December 31, 1970
76. Brian McDonnell, February 16, 1970
77. Richard P. Radetich, June 19, 1970
78. Harold L. Hamilton, October 19, 1970
79. Charles D. Logasa, February 11, 1971
80. Arthur D. O'Guinn, July 30, 1971
81. John V. Young, August 29, 1971
82. Code W. Beverly, January 24, 1972
83. Michael Herring, September 19, 1974
84. Joseph W. Boswell, May 3, 1977
85. Douglas E. Gibbs, November 27, 1977
86. Robert E. Hooper, February 9, 1978
87. Vernon McDowell, 1981
88. John S. Macaulay, July 17, 1982
89. James W. Bloesch, August 3, 1988
90. John J. Blessing, November 15, 1989
91. Isiah Nelson III, April 19, 1990
92. James L. Gueff, November 15, 1994
93. George Stasko, January 16, 1999
94. Kirk Brookbush, January 11, 2000
95. James Dougherty, January 11, 2000
96. Jon Cook, June 12, 2002
97. Isaac Espinoza, April 10, 2004

Of the 97 officers killed in the line of duty, 59 were shot (one by his own brother), 11 died in motorcycle accidents, 11 in auto accidents, 2 were stabbed, 3 died in helicopter accidents, 2 in streetcar accidents, 2 in brawls, 2 in accidental shootings, 1 by heart failure, 1 in a fall, 1 in an earthquake, and 1 directing traffic. One motorcycle officer died going to Candlestick Park and another died coming back from the Stick. Approximately 14 of the murders are unsolved.

Striking examples of concern for fellow man and duty to the job are exhibited in two deaths. In 1932 Patrolman William E. Manning worked the graveyard shift in the Mission and observed a holdup of a streetcar. The robber emptied his gun into Manning, who then crawled a block on his hands and knees and threw his revolver through a window to summon help. His first words were, "There is a wounded man down the street, someone should call for help, he is worst off than me." Manning later died of his injuries in the hospital. In 1925 Patrolman George Campbell was shot, yet still handcuffed a bank robber and asked a grocerman to phone home to tell his mother he would not be able to bring home the vegetables that night and not to worry. He died a few hours later. His killer went to San Quentin.

Two stars were involved in the department's 1994 fatal shooting of an officer and in the next fatal shooting of an officer in 2004. In 1994 James Guelff, star 1461, was murdered and John Payne, star 64, was injured. In 2004, Isaac Espinoza, star 64, was murdered and Barry Parker, star 1461, was injured. It is usually the tradition of the SFPD to retire the star of the fallen officer; however, Guelff's star was mistakenly not retired, which allowed this unusual event.

These officers' names are on the Memorial Wall at the Hall of Justice at 850 Bryant, first floor; at the California Peace Officers Memorial outside the state capitol in Sacramento; and at the National Law Enforcement Officers Memorial in Washington. These memorials also have websites with online tributes. One of the goals of this author is to ensure all photos of these officers and the line of duty narrative are available on these sites.

BIBLIOGRAPHY

Allen, Terence B. *San Francisco Coroner's Office: A History 1850–1980.* Redactors Press, 1999.

Ashabranner, Brent. *Badge of Valor: The National Law Enforcement Officers Memorial.* Twenty-First Century Books, 2000.

Dillon, Richard H. *San Francisco's Brotherhood of Blood: The Hatchet Men.* Comstock Editions, 1962.

Dempsey, Thomas G. *Men of Courage: San Francisco Police Officers.* Cedar Publishing, 1998.

——. *True Stories That Cops Tell to One Another.* Cedar Publishing, 1998.

Dickensheet, Dean W. *Great Crimes of San Francisco: True Tales of Intrigue by the Bay.* Comstock Editions, 1974.

Graysmith, Robert. *The Sleeping Lady: The Trailside Murders Above the Golden Gate.* Onyx Books, 1991.

Graysmith, Robert. *Zodiac.* Berkley Books, 1987.

Hansen, Gladys C. and Frank R. Quinn. *Behind the Silver Star: An Account of the San Francisco Police Department.* San Francisco Public Library, 1981.

Hill, Andrew. "A Chilling Interview with Sara Jane Moore: 'The Real Reason I Tried to Kill President Ford.' " *Playboy.* p. 69.

Howard, Clark. *Zebra.* Berkley Publishing Group, 1980.

Mullen, Kevin J. *Let Justice Be Done: Crime and Politics in Early San Francisco.* University of Nevada Press, 1989.

Rush. *Confessions of an Ex-Secret Service Agent.* Pocket Books, 1991.

SFPD. "The Watch Report: SFPD 150 Years of Service." August 1999.

http://www.sfgov.org/site/police_index.asp

Pickelhaupt, Bill. *Shanghaied in San Francisco.* Flyblister Press, 1997.

To participate in the new Oral History program for retired SFPD members, please email author John Garvey at discusthrower@comcast.net. Audio and digital video will be made and donated to the planned reactivated SFPD Museum and to the City of San Francisco Public Library History Room at the Main Library, by author. Together let's preserve more SFPD history and retain these unique stories for future generations.

A portion of the proceeds of each book will be donated to the National Law Enforcement Officers Memorial Fund, Inc., (NLEMF) in Washington, DC. The author plans to work on ensuring that photos of all fallen SFPD officers are placed online on the NLEMF website; along with the State of California and City of San Francisco Memorial websites. In addition, he plans to work as a private citizen to help reinstitute the SFPD Museum in the City, and via the Internet, so everyone can continue to enjoy this remarkable history of police service by the SFPD.